Elementary Physical Education
Curriculum Guide
For Today's Physical Education Teacher

Dr. Martha Higgins

PublishAmerica
Baltimore

First printing

At the specific preference of the author, PublishAmerica allowed this work to remain exactly as the author intended, verbatim, without editorial input.

ISBN: 1-4241-1328-8
PUBLISHED BY PUBLISHAMERICA, LLLP
www.publishamerica.com
Baltimore

Printed in the United States of America

Acknowledgements

Appreciation and gratitude are extended to my family, friends and colleagues for their support, encouragement and understanding. A special thanks to Mrs. Wellington for her assistance., also a special thank you to my nieces and nephews who played many of the games that are located in this book.

Physical Activity and Fitness Quote

"Significant adults are primed to structure the environment and exhibit behaviors that enhance children's physical competency, beliefs, self-esteem, and enjoyment of physical activity. In turn, these perceptions and emotions are the keys to solving the mystery of motivating kids in physical activity".

President's Council on Physical Fitness & Sports

Foreword

In order to meet the wellness needs of the youth of the 21st century, physical education curriculums must consist of a body of organized knowledge that not only addresses the physical domain of individuals but must also examine the societal and cultural aspects as well. This curriculum guide was written based on that concept. Appropriate curriculums for physical education students are needed to improve the short-term and long-term health status of our nation's children especially those from underserved, ethnically diverse, low-income groups.

Behaviors and attitudes regarding physical activity patterns are formed early in life, therefore it is necessary to promote the importance of physical activity to children when they are young because high risk behaviors and physiological risk factors are difficult to change once they are established during childhood. This physical education curriculum guide takes account the attitudes and behaviors that children tend to associate with physical activity and physical education class.

All children have the right to reach their potential and this curriculum provides an opportunity for such achievement. for it can be a solid method for implementing a successful physical education program or by adding to an already existing one.

Chapter I
Vision:
Philosophy of Physical Education

Physical education should be a place where students are provided the opportunity to participate in organized activities that both stimulates and challenges the students' physical, emotional, and mental health. Physical education classes should be instructed by a certified physical education teacher who is current in the areas of teaching methods, and learning styles. Physical education classes should be conducted in a safe and healthy environment, one that is conducive to learning.

Physical Education Defined, The Importance of Physical Education

The National Association for Sport and Physical Education (NAPSE)[1] defines physical education as a planned sequential instruction that promotes lifelong physical activity. It is designed to develop basic movement skills, sport skills, and physical fitness as well as to enhance mental, social, and emotional health. Physical education is an integral part of the total education of every child in Kindergarten through 12th grade. Quality physical education programs are needed to increase the physical competence, health-related fitness, self-responsibility and enjoyment of physical activity for all students so that they can be physically active for a lifetime. Physical education programs can only provide these benefits if they are well planned and well implemented.

Data from Langford & Carter (2003)[2], indicate that more than half of U.S. adults do not meet recommended levels of moderate physical activity. Nearly half of young people 12-21 years of age are not vigorously active. Current research has proven that more school-based interventions such as appropriate physical education classes are needed if the goal of increasing the levels of physical activity is going to be met. As of now the most recent recommendations state that children and adults should strive for at least 30 minutes of daily of moderate intensity physical activity.

Walking briskly or biking for pleasure or transportation, swimming, engaging in sports, games, participating in physical education and doing tasks in the home may all contribute to accumulated activity[3]. In addition to being physically active children need to learn fundamental motor skills and develop health related physical fitness. Physical education provided at school, is a great way to encourage activity and develop fitness among children and for many children will be their only preparation for an active lifestyle. For this reason the Centers for Disease Control and Prevention and the National Association of Physical Education and Sport and the American Heart Association all recommend comprehensive daily physical education for children k-12[4].

NAPSE emphasizes how Physical education is important in the life of every child because Physical education has many advantages such as:

Regular, healthful physical activity

Provides a wide-range of developmentally appropriate activities for all children.

Support of other Subject Areas

Reinforces knowledge learned across the curriculum, serves as a lab for application of content in science, math and social studies.

Self Discipline

Facilitates development of student responsibility for health and fitness.

Improved judgment

Quality physical education can influence moral development. Students have the opportunity to assume leadership, cooperate with others; question actions and regulations and accept responsibility for their own behavior.

Strengthened peer relationships

Physical education can be a major force in helping children socialize with others successfully and provides opportunities to learn positive people skills. Especially during late childhood and early adolescence, being able to participate in dances, games and sports is an important part of peer culture.

Improved self-confidence and self-esteem

Physical education instills a stronger sense of self-worth in children based on their mastery of skills and concepts in physical activity. They can become more confident, assertive, independent and self-confident.

Evidence from the Surgeon General Report [5]consistently shows that people of all ages and sizes, both male and female, benefit from regular physical activity and healthy eating as a way to maintain a proper energy balance, which is necessary for achieving and maintaining a healthy weight.

The many benefits of physical activity and fitness are well documented, according to data from the Centers for Disease Control and Prevention, physical activity:

builds and maintains healthy bones and muscles, controls weight, builds lean muscle, reduces fat, reduces blood pressure, and improves glucose control.

decreases the risk of obesity and chronic diseases, cancer, high blood pressure, diabetes, colon cancer, and osteoporosis.

reduces feelings of depression and anxiety and promotes psychological well being.

is related to functional independence of older adults, and quality of life of people of all ages.

Healthy People 2010 [6]determined that there has been little change in the goals set in physical activity for the health of the nation. A continuous effort is needed in order to increase the proportion of adolescents who participate in daily school physical education. The target is 50%, but in 1999 only 29% of students participated in daily physical education. It seems as a nation we still have rather a ways to go. Physical education plays an important role in the education of every child. Physical education can develop the knowledge, attitudes, and skills, behaviors and confidence needed to be physically active for life.

Interrelationship of Physical Education and Academics

Learning is acquiring knowledge or developing the ability to perform new behaviors. It is common to think of learning as something that takes place in school, but much of human learning occurs outside the classroom, and people continue to learn throughout their lives[7]

In addition to health and wellness, preliminary research indicates a direct link between physical activity and improved academic performance. It has been proven that participation in physical activity increases adolescents' self-esteem, as well as physical and mental health. Youths are also are less likely to be regular or heavy smokers or use drugs or alcohol, and more likely to stay in school; have good conduct, high academic achievement, and practice good nutrition habits. Youths receiving additional activity tend to show improved attributes such as increased brain function and nourishment, higher energy concentration levels, changes in body build perceptions and behaviors which may all support cognitive learning[8].

Children learn through many ways. It is important that the physical education curriculum is developed to meet the different learning styles of students. A major thrust in curriculum development in schools today is the integration of subject content across the curriculum. Integration refers to the mutual relationship between subject matter and suggests the building of relationships between all areas of study that make up the school curriculum. Integration of curriculum enhances learning in many ways such as encouraging students to transfer what is learned in one setting to new settings and reinforcing curriculum content by more in-depth exposure to the material. Physical education can be integrated within the regular classroom curriculum through the techniques of The Thematic Approach and the Shared Integration model[9].

The Thematic Approach is a popular technique used to integrate subject areas and include physical activity. In this approach, teachers overlap the content across the curriculum over a set period of time, while focusing on one theme. Another common practice in promoting physical activity through curriculum integration is the Shared Integration Model. A lesson would include two distinct disciplines working together with a focus on the shared concepts. Examples of lesson plans utilizing these integration models can be found in the appendices.

In lieu of the staggering research concerning the health status of school aged children, it is time to focus on physical education as a necessary objective of education, just as we do with other academic areas. In doing so, physical education can play an important role in changing health behaviors as well as improving the pursuit of academic excellence. According to Langford & Carter 2 no other discipline can have more effect upon the physical aspects of the human body, healthy lifestyles, and enjoyable of lifelong activity. As states push for academic excellence, physical education must be required in order to contribute to the individual's well being and avoidance of premature death resulting from physical inactivity.

Teaching Physical Education in the 21st Century

Physical inactivity has become a serious problem in the United States. Inactivity is more prevalent among those with lower income and education, and beginning in adolescence, affects females more than males. A pattern of inactivity also known as Sedentism begins early in life, which can lead to the development of chronic diseases 4. This makes the promotion of physical activity among children somewhat a challenge for the physical education teacher. How can students be expected to meet the standards to acquire the skills and habits they need to lead a healthy life without a gymnasium or a safe place to play?

In order to meet the health needs of the youths of today, leaders in the field of physical education have reorganizes the physical education curriculum into what is now known as the new PE. This curriculum focuses on lifetime physical activity and fitness instead of only sports competition and traditional programs.

For example, Samuels [10]found that Middle school students in Herndon, Virginia use heart rate monitors to measure their aerobic effort during 15 minute fitness runs, while Fukushima[11], indicates how in the St. Paul, Minnesota area, some physical education teachers are using popular activities such as rock-climbing and in-line skating to make physical education more fun.

Children from underserved populations may lack the proper facilities, and funding to sustain such physical education programs. Various resources have been developed to assist in enhancing the physical education program such as the Physical Education Program grant (PEP). However; physical education teachers that serve such populations often find themselves at a great disadvantage in attempting to maintain an adequate program and keep up with standards of the new PE.

This curriculum guide is designed to assist those teachers of elementary children, especially those in disadvantaged populations in addressing the new PE by providing activities and lessons that are designed to meet State and National standards in physical education and physical fitness, focus more on the development of a lifelong healthy lifestyle and positive social and cooperative behaviors including improving physical activity levels and team building skills rather than on competitive sports and are curtailed to the environmental factors that affect these students.

The Centers for Disease Control and Prevention recommends that educators continue to strive to provide quality, preferably daily k-12 physical education classes that promote adolescents' and young adults confidence in their ability to be physically active, and that involve friends, peers, and parents.

Chapter II
The Physical Education Curriculum: Conceptual Framework

This Curriculum Guide is a handbook for educators that provide them with resources and strategies that can be used in the classroom as well as in the gymnasium. The physical education curriculum specifies the level of achievement that a student is expected to attain by means of Content Standards. The NAPSE Content Standard serves as an excellent framework in developing a sound physical education program.

According to NAPSE to pursue a lifetime of healthful physical activity, a physically educated person:

has learned skills necessary to perform a variety of physical activities;

knows the implications of and the benefits from involvement in physical activities;

does participate regularly in physical activity;

is physically fit;

values physical activity and its contribution to a healthful lifestyle.

Physical activity is critical to the development and maintenance of good health. The National goal of physical education is to develop physically educated individuals who have the knowledge, skills, and confidence to enjoy a lifetime of healthful physical activity.

The National Standards for Physical Education are as follows:

Standard 1: Demonstrates competency in motor skills and movement patterns needed to perform a variety of physical activities.

Standard 2: Demonstrates understanding of movement concepts, principles, strategies, and tactics as they apply to the learning and performance activities.

Standard 3: Participates regularly in physical activity.

Standard 4: Achieves and maintain a health-enhancing level of physical fitness.

Standard 5: Exhibits responsible personal and social behavior that respects self and others in physical activity settings.

Standard 6: Values physical activity for health, enjoyment, challenge, self-expression, and and/or social interaction.

Curriculum Goals and Objectives

Program Goals

The goals for this physical education curriculum take into account the needs of the student's physical and social surroundings. The program goals for the physical education curriculum are:

Create and sustain a comprehensive fitness program, which provides activities that can be used through adulthood.

Develop problem solving and social skills.

Maintain positive self-esteem through participation in various movement activities that enhance and foster success.

Identify resources that are available within the community that provide opportunity to engage in physical activity.

Program Objectives

The program objectives for this curriculum furthers the development of the three domains of physical education: psychomotor, cognitive and affective.

To enable students to experience fundamental movement skills that contributes to overall health and well being.

To develop knowledge, skills, and attitudes that allows students to participate in lifelong physical activity.

To acquire knowledge of safety practices and procedures and develop an overall awareness of safety.

To provide an environment that enables each child to acquire the necessary knowledge and skills that fosters social development.

This curriculum is divided into content areas under which the curriculum will function. The three major content areas are: the Developmental Model, the Movement model, and the Wellness Model. The activities have been arranged by levels of development (grades k-2) and (grades 3-5) for instruction. In order to ensure that lessons are worthwhile for students they should be introduced to students in a manner that allows for success. Development includes skills such as hand apparatus, games, sports, stunts, and tumbling and fitness activities. Children learn in different styles and at different paces, so they will vary regarding the timing in which they will become competent at certain skills; therefore activities are placed in different levels in order to motivate teachers to introduce activities to children that are appropriate.

The Movement Model

Human movement plays an important role in physical education program. Movement teaches children the concepts of space, balance, and force. This component of the curriculum includes fundamental skills of locomotor, walk, run, hop, skip, slide, leap, dodge, and change direction. Non-locomotor skills such as bend, twist, reach, lift, raise, lower, turn, curl, stretch and balance. Manipulative skills such as throw, catch, volley, and kick. Body management – control of body on floor, in flight, balance, coordination and spatial awareness. Children should be provided the opportunity to participate in the many forms of movement.

17

Wellness Model

Students need to know how to maximize their health by understanding how the mind and body function, and how to responsible for their own actions and behaviors. For the purpose of this curriculum, wellness is considered multidimensional, involving the whole person's relation to the total environment. This component involves teaching children identification of body parts, understanding how eating and exercising go hand-in-hand, how physical inactivity and obesity are related and how coping skills and decision making skills are important in teaching children to make the most of their overall health.

Chapter III
Learning Environment:
Teaching Physical Education
in the classroom

There will be times when the physical education teacher will be required to conduct physical education class in the classroom. This could be due to special events and programs that require the use of the gymnasium. The physical education class may be conducted outdoors, however if weather does not permit, then the use of a classroom or multi-purpose room is necessary.

Providing physical education in the classroom comes with its many restrictions, such as the availability of space. A benefit of conducting physical education in the classroom is that it provides an excellent opportunity for students to further their knowledge regarding wellness. Cooperative games are an integral part of the lesson plan but should not be the only activities offered.

All efforts should be made to ensure that when the physical education class is conducted in the classroom, the effectiveness of the programs should not weaken and some form of physical fitness is offered to students. Physical education rituals and routines should be maintained when the gymnasium is not available.

The noise level should be kept to a minimum as to not interfere with other classes. If chairs and desks have to be moved all efforts should be made to maintain order. Consideration of others property, replacing chairs and desks when done and safety procedures should be discussed. Students should be careful when moving about the room and around the desks and chairs. Proper ventilation should also be maintained, the floor should be free of objects and litter. Equipment necessary for conducting physical education class should be kept on a cart for easy access. Lesson plans should be developed that coincide with the classroom environment, this ensures that the right equipment is used and a safe climate is maintained.

Activities should be designed so that waiting time is kept to a minimum. The activities section of this curriculum provides examples of some classroom activities that can be used. Developmental and movement concepts should not be compromised because physical education has to be conducted in spaces other the gymnasium. The classroom can be a valuable asset in the implementation of a physical education program.

Facilities

In order to maintain a quality physical education program an adequate facility is necessary. The out door facility include an appropriate playground area that is free of objects and safety hazards, has proper padding and all apparatus is in good order. The indoor facility in elementary physical education often consists of a gymnasium/cafeteria that makes use for physical education a problem at times. Scheduling conflicts arise because the gymnasium cannot be used usually the hour preceding lunch and the hour after lunch.

The National Association for Sport and Physical Education (NAPSE) has established guidelines for facilities, equipment and instructional materials in Elementary Physical Education.

Guidelines for Facilities

Boards of Education, through their school budget process, fund: the purchase and maintenance of appropriate and sufficient physical education supplies and equipment; and equitable physical education facilities and maintenance of these facilities for each school. Physical education teachers, physical education program administrator, and school administrators should jointly:

a) develop standards for appropriate supplies and equipment; and procedures for purchasing. provide input to plans for new physical education facilities.

3. School and community facilities and programs are designed and implemented to support and complement one another in serving children's needs.

4. There is a dedicated facility for the physical education instructional program.

5. Adequate space, ranging from 110 sq. ft. to 150 sq. ft. per child, for learning movement activities in which children can move freely and safety. The student/teacher ratio should be 25; 1 per class. Intact classes should not interfere with one another.

6. Adequate space ranging from 400 to 600 sq. ft. with a height of 12' – 15", is available for safe and proper storage of physical equipment.

7. Physical activity space is designed to facilitate instruction free of distractions and' pass through traffic patterns'.

8. Restrooms and drinking fountains should be located close to the instructional facilities, if drinking fountains are in the instructional area they should be recessed.

9. Office space, ranging from 120 to 240 sq. ft. in size, for the physical education teacher is provided to allow students convenient address to their teacher for consultation and/or assistance.

10. A learning environment with adequate acoustics ('sound baffles') permits children to safely participate in all phases of instruction.

11. Indoor facilities, with proper flooring and lighting, are clean and sanitized on a daily basis. Floor surface should be either hardwood with cushion, or a roll out synthetic product. The minimum amount of light should be 30-foot candles.

12. All-weather outdoor surfaces are properly marked with circles, lines, courts, etc. to permit participation in a wide variety of activities and are appropriate for students with varied ability levels.

13. Outdoor areas are available for teaching and:

are free from safety hazards (such as glass, debris, water).
located away from occupied classrooms.
have clearly defined physical boundaries,
are far away from parking lots or streets {i.e., no closer than 100 yards}, or are separated by barriers that prevent vehicles from entering the area.
are close enough to school building to permit access to equipment, and provide shelter in case of inclement weather.

14. Natural play areas are available to facilitate and encourage creative and exploratory play.

Every elementary school includes indoor physical education facilities configured as either a gymnasium or a multi-purpose room. The gymnasium or multi-purpose room should measure approximately 70 x 100' feet with a maximum of 110 square feet allotted per child.

The primary use of the indoor facility is for physical education instruction. If the indoor facility is used for other purposes (e.g., school lunches, school convocations) the instructional program in physical education should be scheduled to maximize use of the facility for instructional time.

An excellent reference for the logistics of a facility is provided by Pangrazi. It is of utmost importance that the gymnasium be free from potential safety hazards (such as protruding structures). If the gymnasium also serves as a cafeteria, lunch tables should be recessed into walls. Boundaries of the gymnasium should be clearly defined to exclude the area in which tables or other equipment is stored. There should be a minimum of 7-9 foot area between stored items and the instructional area.

The flooring of the gymnasium should be kept clean. Safe flooring surfaces include hardwood or tile with adequate cushioning or a synthetic composition that gas a resilient surface. Floor markings facilitate a variety of activities, but the number of different markings (e.g., lines, circles, shapes) should be limited. Temporary markings for specific purposes should be removed when no longer needed[12].

Wall and ceiling acoustical treatments should be included to create adequate sound quality. Children should be able to fully participate in physical education activities and simultaneously hear their peers and teacher at all times. The gymnasium should be well lighted (minimum of 30 foot candles) and free from shadows. Lights should be covered with protective grids. The ceiling should be a minimum of 20' and illumination should be sufficient to facilitate the instructional program (e.g., ball handling activities: striking with the body; striking with paddles; volleyball). Gymnasium walls should have a smooth or flat surface from the floor up to 10 or 15 feet of height. Walls can then be used for a variety of instructional purposes (e.g., using the wall to throw toward or to strike toward). The indoor physical education facility should have easy access to outdoor instructional areas in order to facilitate quick transitions to outdoor facilities.

Equipment and Supplies

Appropriate equipment and supplies are needed in order to maintain a sound physical education program. Appendix 2 provides an example of an equipment list. This list provides a foundation for an elementary curriculum based on the National Standards for Physical Education. Skill themes (i.e., throwing, catching, kicking, striking, bouncing, jumping/landing, skipping, etc.) and movement concepts (i.e., spatial, effort and relationship awareness) establish the base for educational game, dance, and gymnastic experiences. The size, texture, weight, and/or color of equipment should be varied to accommodate children's level of motor development and physical growth. Colors can also be used for organizational and instructional purposes.

The basic list stipulates the instructional material that should be available for teaching. In addition, extra basic-list items should be held in storage for replacement during the year. Optional supplies depend on personal preferences and available funds. How does a physical education teacher decide what you need? First, think about what you will teach and what you have on hand. Next, prioritize the list so that those things you need most often are at the top of the list. Finally consider budget and storage issues. Buy what you will use most frequently and is within your budget and that you have room to store. Each year, add to the equipment on hand, remembering to replace items that you need to be replaced because of wear and tear. An accurate inventory of equipment should be undertaken at the start and at the end of each school year. Through a sound inventory system the durability of equipment and supplies and an accounting of supplies lost or misplaced can be established. The ordering of supplies and equipment should be done by the end of the school year or earlier, if possible. A delivery date in late August or September should be specified so that orders can be checked and any necessary adjustments made before the school year begins.

Storage of Equipment

Adequate storage space must be given careful thought. {400 to 600 sq. ft.; 12'-15' height). Storage areas are planned to allow for adequate space with reasonable ease of access to needed equipment. All physical education equipment should be marked for purposes of keeping an updated inventory and to guard against loss or theft. Equipment used by classroom teachers and or for recess should be kept separate from the physical education inventory 14.

Consider the size of the children, class, and facility when deciding the appropriateness of an activity for that facility. When selecting equipment consider the size, ability, and age of the students and the match of equipment to the intended learning outcome. Prevent injuries by regular maintenance of equipment and facilities and appropriate supervision allowing students both structured and unstructured opportunities to learn and create when using gross motor skills is an important part of child development. Being safe means reducing risks as much as possible 14.

Assessment

It is no longer acceptable to evaluate children entirely on a single standard test. The purpose of assessment is to determine whether progress is being made toward learning objectives established for students. Evaluation should review all phases of physical education including pupil progress, teacher performance and program effectiveness. Student evaluation can be formal or informal and can focus on individual or group progress 15. Teacher evaluation can be used to improve the instructional process or to secure data for measuring teacher effectiveness. Program evaluation is used to examine the total program or selected program areas. Approaches and curriculum that are effective need to be retained and enhanced and what are deficient needs to be corrected.

Methods of Assessment

Once of the purposes of the evaluation have been clearly defined, the measurement techniques to be used are selected. The teacher may choose observational techniques or more formal skill and written tests. The instrument may be *norm-referenced* or *criterion-referenced*. In norm-referenced measures the scores may be compared with the scores of other children of similar 'ages and sex. Fitness tests are examples of norm-referenced tests. Information from such tests is qualitative, it is a numerical score of what the children did, for example, how fast they ran or how far they threw. From their test results, percentiles or other standard test norms are computed. Criterion-referenced measures may be quantitative or qualitative In quantitative measures the teacher establishes some criterion for the class to reach – perhaps it is 30 sit-ups, a standing jump of five feet, or some other quantitative performance standard. Qualitative criterion measures how a person performed rather than the result of that effort.

Qualitative criterion – referenced information is helpful in determining errors in performance important to improving the effectiveness of skill and also in looking at behaviors that do not lend themselves to a norm, such as certain social behaviors 15.

Another way to use the criterion referenced method for assessment for grading is by setting performance standards. Performance standards are pre-established criteria that must be met to receive a particular grade. Performance based objectives are important part of the curriculum building process. The norm and criterion referenced approaches to evaluation are the two most common methods used to assess students. The following sections describe six approaches to assessments. The use of any of these approaches is situation specific and depends on the experience and skill of the teacher[13].

Student Self Evaluation

It is important for physical education to provide children with the requisite levels of fitness skill, and knowledge to voluntarily participate in physical activity and assume an active lifestyle. An important ingredient in the successful attainment of this goal is the evaluation process. Youths should be given the opportunity to conduct self-evaluation. Students who are able to evaluate their personal level of performance are more likely to be active participants in physical than those who cannot. It becomes increasingly important to teach students how to assess their abilities in relationship to performance-based objectives. Once this procedure is established, it becomes possible to integrate a self-evaluation scheme into a grading system 16.

Teacher Observation

This is a commonly used method commonly used in assessing pupil performance. Observation in this context offers a way to compare the performances of children of the same age and experienced. For observations to be useful several observations should made within a lesson and in several lessons 16. Since elementary school children's performance may not be consistent, observations focusing on the lesson objectives help the teacher determine what feedback is necessary and what further emphasis is needed.

Skills Test

Skills test may be used to assess student's performance. These may be standardized tests found in the literature or teacher made tests. Examples of teacher made tests include measuring the distance of a long jump, or the time in the 50-yard dash 16. In administration of a skill tests every effort should be made to maximize the activity for all children and to organize the testing so a minimum amount of tune is needed. Often other techniques are more efficient of time and permit the children more activity than formal skill testing.

Authentic Assessment

This assessment is integrated with the teaching effort and provides meaningful information about student learning and achievement 16. This style of assessment is accomplished by focusing on student outcomes and refers to assessment tasks in which students demonstrate skills and competencies rather than selecting one of several predetermined answers.

In recent years, the call for accountability in all facets of education has been clear. In response to this demand the National Association of Sport and Physical Education (NAPSE) sponsored a project (1992) resulting in Outcomes of Quality Physical Education that includes 20 outcomes statements culminating in a definition of a physically educated person. Follow-up work to the Outcomes Project has been the development and adoption of the Moving into the Future: National Physical Education Standards: A Guide to Content and Assessment (1995).

Content standards from this document are shown at the beginning of chapter three. Content standards specify what students should know and be able to do and are roughly equal to 'student learning outcomes' or student objectives. These content standards, sample benchmarks and assessment examples have been developed for grade k-12, at two-year intervals. A major benefit of comprehensive standards and accompanying assessments is that they provide strong rational that physical education is not "academically soft" The standards show the uninformed that there are meaningful and important areas of achievement in physical education and that these levels of achievement can be measured. An example of assessment strategies can be found in the appendix.

Portfolio Assessment

This is a type of authentic assessment that offers a visual presentation of student's performance, including their strengths and areas for improvement. Portfolios are used in the physical education assessment process. 15. Physical education can maintain records of fitness progress, demonstrated skill competencies, physical activity behavior, and social interactive behavior. Teachers can utilize video technology to document performances and assist in evaluation and computer technology to record, store, and report this valuable information.

Parental Reports

This report provides a record of student participation of some form of out-of-class performance. These reports may refer to play choices purposeful practice, formal activities such as sports clubs or lessons in a sport or family activity 16. They can include anecdotal information and the signature of the person who observed the out of class performance.

Student Journals

Student journals provide a student record of participation, results, feelings, and perceptions about events. Entries are made on a regular basis and can serve as indicators of success, failure, enjoyment, or other products of participation 16. Entries are judged as right or wrong as students describe both positive and negative feelings. Self-analysis and reflections are often included.

The alternative assessment techniques described in the section are examples of a variety of alternative assessments methods presented in the NAPSE (1995) document. All alternative assessment techniques should be characterized by the following:

tasks that directly examine behavior the teacher wishes to measure

a focus on product and quality of performance
Criterion-referenced scoring
assessment of higher levels of learning
student participation in development of the assessment and ownership of the final product
assessment criteria that are given to students in advance.

Future research is warranted to extend understanding about and improve methods for enhancing ways to promote physical activity and physical fitness. Techniques that enable educators to match interventions and develop curriculum to effectively meet the needs of the nations' youth are clearly needed. Curricula that are geared toward specific populations, rather than general in nature should be developed and implemented.

Chapter IV
Developmental k-2

Apparatus Activities
Activities with parachutes
Exercise Activities
*Exercise should be done vigorously and with enough repetitions to challenge the children. In addition to the exercises presented, others can be adapted to parachute play.

Toe Toucher

Focus/Skill: gripping – overhand, underhand, one hand and two handgrips, fitness and strength development.

Procedure/Play: Students sit with feet extended under the parachute and hold the chute with a two-hand grip, drawing it up to the chin. Bend forward and touch the grip to the toes. Return parachute to stretched position.

Equipment: One parachute large enough for up to 30 children.

Teaching Idea: extend the body under the parachute in curl-up position, so that the chute comes up to the chin when held taut. Do curl-ups, returning each time to the stretched chute position.

Dorsal Lift

Focus/Skill: gripping, strength development.
Procedure/Play: Lie in a prone position, with head toward the parachute and feet pointed back, away from it. Grip the chute and slide toward the feet until there is some tension on it. Raise the chute off the ground with a vigorous lift of the arms, until head and chest rise off the ground. Return.
Teaching Idea: Have students perform this a certain number of times.

V-Sit

Focus/Skill: Agility, coordination and strength development.
Procedure/Play: Lie supine, with head toward the parachute. Do V-ups by raising the upper and lower parts of the body simultaneously into a V-shaped position. The knees should be kept straight.

Backward Pull

Focus/Skill: pulling, coordination and strength development.
Procedure/Play: Face the parachute and pull back, away from its center. Pulls can be made from a sitting, kneeling, or standing position.
Teaching Idea: With arm flexed, do side pulls with either arm. Other variations of pulling can be used.

Lights Out

Focus/Skill: gripping, strength development, and agility.
Procedure/Play: Children begin by making a dome. The parachute is on the floor, holding with two hands and kneeling on one knee the children stand up quickly, thrusting their arms above the head and then return to the starting position, take two steps toward

the center and sit inside the chute. The chute can be held with the hands at the side or by sitting on it.

Teaching Idea: Some or all of the children can change to the inside of the parachute on the down movement. Domes can also be made while moving in a circle.

Mushroom Release

Focus/Skill: strength development, coordination

Procedure/Play: All children release at the peak of inflation and either run out from under the chute or move to the center and sit down, with the parachute descending on top of them.

Teaching Idea: Have the children make a mushroom. As soon as they move into the center, they release holds and run once around the inside of the parachute, counterclockwise, back to place.

Popcorn

Focus/Skill: strength development of arms, hands, shoulder.

Equipment: Beanbags

Procedure/Play: Have children hold parachute with two hands at waist level. Place a number of beanbags (from six to ten) on the parachute. Shake the parachute to make the beanbags rise like corn popping.

Teaching Idea: Substitute small balls, such as whiffle balls, foam, or fleece balls. Have children count every time a ball is popped off the parachute.

Cageball Elevator

Focus/Skill: coordination, agility

Procedure/Play: A two-foot cage ball is placed on the parachute. On command, the class elevates the chute and allows it to make a mushroom. Just before the chute with the ball on it reaches its apex, youngsters drop the chute to the floor.

Equipment: 1 Cage ball per parachute.

Teaching Idea: Done correctly the cage ball should be elevated to the ceiling. Have students complete a set number of repetitions in order to get the maximum out of the activity.

Hole in one

Focus/Skill: gripping, agility, coordination.

Procedure/Play: Use four or more plastic whiffle balls the size of golf balls. The balls should be of two different colors. The class is divided into two teams on opposite sides of the parachute. The object is to shake the other teams' ball into the hole in the center of the parachute.

Equipment: Whiffle balls the size of golf balls.

Teaching Idea: Minimize competition by setting a specific time such as three minutes, at that time Teacher counts each teams number of balls that were shaken into center hole of the parachute, add them together and announce total number to class.

Number Game

Focus/Skill: Cardiovascular endurance, strength, agility.

Procedure/Play: The students around the parachute count off by fours, then they run lightly, holding the parachute in one hand. The teacher calls out one of the numbers. Students with that number immediately release their grip on the parachute and run forward to the next place vacated. They must put on a burst of speed to move ahead.

Teaching Idea: The parachute should be kept at a safe pace so that children don't stumble or fall in attempt to keep up.

Activities with Gymnasium Scooters

*Gymnasium scooters make excellent devices for developmental activity when used properly. An important rule in the use of scooters is that children are not to stand on scooters as they would on skateboards.

Bring It Home

Procedure/Play: The students are evenly divided, lined up on each side of the gymnasium and given a number. The teacher calls out a number, and the players from each team with that number comes out. They are on opposite ends of each other. On signal they each use their scooters to move to their respective half court line to retrieve their bean bag and get back safely across their end line within a certain amount of time.

Focus/Skill: Agility, coordination, endurance.

Equipment: Bean bags, 1 per team

Teaching Idea: Minimize competition by setting a time limit in which you know both players will safely cross end line with time to spare. Students are placed on opposite end lines of each other to reduce injuries, such as clashing into each and rolling over classmate fingers that is likely to occur when beanbags are placed side by side.

Scooter Cage ball

Focus/Skill: gripping, agility, and coordination.

Equipment: 1 cage ball

Procedure/Play: Students are lined up evenly on each side the gymnasium. One cage ball is placed in the center. On command students move to the ball on their scooters. The object is to move the ball to the opposite wall by punching it with the fist.

Teaching Idea: Place one student on each end to act as goalie. Only goalie is allowed to catch ball or allowed get off scooter to retrieve ball and put back into play.

Scooter Freeze Tag

Focus/Skill: coordination, agility, and endurance.
Procedure/play: Students are scattered throughout gymnasium on their scooter in sitting position. One person is designated to be "it". On command, "it" attempts to tag students. Those tagged are frozen and cannot move unless touched (unfrozen) by another teammate who has not been tagged. Any students caught moving after being frozen pays a penalty.
Teaching Idea: Specify the level at which the students must freeze. Use different students to be "it".

Scooter Relays

Focus/Skill: agility, coordination, and endurance.
Equipment: 1 "6-12" cone
Procedure/Play: Students are lined up on scooters single file on opposite end of court facing each other. On command, the first student in line one goes over to line two tagging that student and moving to the end of that line. The student in line two, who has been tagged, moves on to line one and tags the student and goes to the end of line one. It continues on until the last student in each line has been tagged. When done correctly the students in line one end up in line two and the students in line two end up in line one.
Teaching Idea: Change positions that each child can take on the scooter. Possible positions include kneeling, sitting, or on tummy.

Scooter Lane Relays

Focus/Skill: endurance, agility, and coordination.
Equipment: 1 '6-12' cone
Procedure/Play: Students are on scooters in sitting position divided into groups that are in lane formation. Lanes will be 10-15 feet apart. The first player from each lane moves forward, around turning point (which can be a cone) and back to their team. Player

repeats the trip with second player in tow. Player repeats the trip until entire group moves around the turning point and returns to the starting line. The process is repeated until the entire team moves around the turning point and returns to the starting lines.

Teaching Idea: Try different positions such as kneeling, or on stomach.

Scooter Indian Club Relay

Focus/Skill: gripping, strength development, and agility.

Equipment: Hula-hoops, Indians clubs, bowling pins or cones.

Procedure/Play: Approximately 15-20 feet in front of each group three Indian clubs are set in a hula hoop The first player from each group moves on the scooter in a sitting position and knocks down club, one at a time, second player from each group moves and stands clubs up, one at a time. Continue until everyone has taken a turn.

Scooter Position Relay

Focus/Skill: strength development, agility, and coordination.

Procedure/Play: Students are divided into three groups and are in lanes sitting on scooters. They are facing three groups on opposite end of court. On command one player at a time from each group moves on the scooter to the opposite end, tags that player and goes to the end of the line. That player who was just tagged moves to the opposite line but in a different position (stomach) and tags that person and goes to the end of the line. The players alternate scooter position per tag. The object is for every one to return back to original starting position.

Scooter Circle Relay

Focus/Skill: Agility, coordination, muscular strength.

Procedure/Play: Students are divided into two groups in circle formation sitting on scooters. Each player from each group is given a number. Teacher calls out a given number, player moves out of circle from each group and all the way around the outside of circle and returns to their starting position. That player must circle all players before they can return to their spot.

Teaching Idea: Positions can be varied, such as kneeling or on stomach. Students should be reminded of scooter safety issues.

Scooter Individual Relay

Focus/Skill: Coordination, agility, strength.

Procedure/Skill: Students are divided into groups and are sitting on their scooter in lanes. One player at a time from each group moves to a turning point and back. Repeat until all players are back in original starting position.

Teaching Idea: Positions may be varied such as kneeling or on stomach.

Scooter Obstacle Course

Focus/Skill: Coordination, strength, agility.

Equipment: Cones, floor tape, Indian clubs or bowling pins.

Procedure/Play: Students are arranged in groups of four sitting on scooters at the beginning of the obstacle courses. The task is described and demonstrated by teacher. A student from each group comes up one at a time and moves through their course. Repeat until all have gone and returned to starting point. The first obstacle is cones set up in a figure 8, next is traveling around hula hoops that have been set up, they then move through the bean bag patch, bean bags have been scattered throughout the path of the scooter, the students picks up a bean bag as they move along to the next person waiting.

Physical Fitness Activities

*A sound fitness development program should be provided as

part of the physical education curriculum. This should be a culmination of activities that embody the physical fitness components. The components of physical fitness are: Cardiovascular endurance, body composition, flexibility, muscular strength and endurance, agility, balance, coordination, power and speed.

Firefighter

Focus/Skill: running, cardiovascular endurance.

Procedure/Play: A fire chief runs around the outside of a circle of children and taps a number of them on the back, saying "Firefighter" each time. After making the round of the circle, the chief goes to the center. When that player says "Fire" the firefighters run around the circle and back to place. The one who returns first and is able to stand in place motionless is picked as the new chief.

Teaching Idea: Vary the selection so that different people are chosen to be fire chief. Also other words can be used to trick the students, but they can only run on the word *fire*. Have the students in the circle sound the siren as the firefighters run.

The Scarecrow and the Crows

Focus/Skill: running, agility, cardiovascular endurance.

Procedure/Play: The students form a large circle representing a garden, which one player is designated the scarecrow, guards. From six to eight crows scatter on the outside of the circle, and the scarecrow assumes a characteristic pose inside the circle. The circle children raise their joined hands and let the crows run through, into the garden, where they pretend to eat. The scarecrow tries to tag the crows. The students in the circle help the crows by raising their joined hands, and allowing them to leave the circle, but they try to hinder the scarecrow. If the scarecrow runs out of the circle, all the crows immediately run into the garden and start to nibble at the vegetables, while the students in the circle hinder the scarecrow's reentry. When the scarecrow has caught one or two crows, a new group of children is selected.

39

Teaching Idea: When the scarecrow has caught one or two crows, a new group of Students are selected. If, after a reasonable period of time, the scarecrow has failed to catch any crows, a change should be made.

Midnight

Focus/Skill: running, cardiovascular endurance

Procedure/Play: A safety line is established about 40 feet from a den in which one Player, the fox, is standing. The others stand behind the safety line and move forward Slowly, asking, "Please Mr. Fox, what time is it?" The fox answers in various fashions such as "Bedtime" "Pretty Late", "Three-Thirty". The fox continues to draw the players toward him. At some point, he answers the question by saying "Midnight" and then chases the others back to the safety line. Any player who is caught joins the fox in the den and helps to catch others. No player in the den may leave, however, until the fox calls out "Midnight".

Teaching Idea: Lane Wolf. The wolf is lame and advances in a series of three running steps and a hop. Other player's chant: "lame wolf can't catch me". The wolf may give chase at any time. Children who are caught must join the wolf and must also move as if lame.

Button My Shoe

Focus/Skill: running, cardiovascular endurance.

Procedure/Play: Two parallel lines are drawn about 50 feet apart. One child is the leader and stands to one side. The rest of the students are behind one of the lines. The leader says, "Ready". The following dialogue takes place between the leader and the students.

Children: One, two.

Leader: Button my shoe.

Children Three four.

Leader: Close the door.

Children: Five, six.

Leader: Pick up sticks.

Children: Seven, eight.

Leader: Run, or you'll be late.

As the students carry on the conversation with the leader, they toe the line, ready to run.

When the leader says the word late, the students run to the other line and return. The first child across the original line gets to be the new leader. The leader can give the last response :(Run, or you'll be late!") in any timing she wishes—pausing or dragging out the words. No child is to leave before the word late is said.

Aviator

Focus/Skill: running, cardiovascular endurance, agility.

Procedure/Play: Players are parked (in push-up position) at one end of the playing area. The air traffic controller (ATC) is in front of the players and calls out, "Aviators, aviators, take off!" Youngsters take off and move like airplanes to the opposite side of the area. The first person to move to the other side and land the plane (get into push-up position facing the ATC) is declared the new ATC.

Teaching Idea: Have the ATC call out some type of stormy weather (lightning, thunder, hurricane and tornado). When the ATC calls out some type of stormy weather, all planes must return o the starting line and resume the parked position. ATC is allowed to give stormy weather warnings once.

Forest Ranger

Focus/Skill: running, cardiovascular endurance.

Procedure/Play: Half of the children form a circle and face the center. These are the trees. The other half of the children is forest rangers and stand behind the trees. An extra student, the forest lookout, is in the center. The forest lookout starts the game by calling, "Fire in the forest. Run, run, run!" Immediately, the forest rangers run around the outside of the circle to the right. After a few moments, the lookout steps in front of one of the trees. This is the signal for each of the rangers to step in front of a tree. One player is left out, and they become the new forest lookout. The trees become rangers and the rangers become trees. Each time the game is played, the circle must be moved out somewhat, because the formation narrows when the rangers step in front of the trees.

Mousetrap

Focus/Skill: running, agility, and coordination.

Procedure/Play: Half of the children form a circle with hands joined and face the center. This is the trap, these children are the cats. The other children are on the outside of the circle. These are the mice. Three signals are given for the game. These can be word cues or signal (usually a whistle). On signal the mice run in and out of the circle, while the cats chant, "in and

out of the mouse trap". On the second signal, the trap snaps shut, cats join hands. All mice caught inside join the circle. The game is repeated until all or most of the mice are caught. The players then exchange places, and the game starts again.

Teaching Idea: A player should not run in and out of the trap through adjacent openings. The game can be played with a parachute. The chute drops down and traps the mice.

Animal Walk

Focus/Skill: Muscular strength, endurance, and flexibility.

Equipment: Prepared cards

Procedure/Play: On colored sheets of 81/2 x 11 paper, write the names of various animal walks and/or draw a picture of the movements/animal. Randomly place the cards around the facility. Have the students move to open areas and get ready to move.

On the start signal, all students begin to "kangaroo jump" around the playing area.

On the stop signal, students move to the nearest card and begin to perform the animal walk listed towards the next card.

Upon reaching the next card, the student's change to the animal walk noted and moves to another card.

This rotation continues for 60 seconds. After that time, students begin to "kangaroo jump" for 30 seconds.

This cycle can be repeated depending on the physical ability of the students.

Teaching Idea: Eliminate the "kangaroo jump" at the beginning of the activity. Have students move directly to an activity card and begin to move from card to card using the appropriate animal movement.

Color Challenge

Focus/Skill: Fitness development and movement competency.

Equipment: Hoops, task cards.

Procedure/Play: A series of movement-oriented task cards is placed in hula-hoops spaced randomly around the facility. Students alternate activities from each task card. Place different colored hula-hoops or other markers randomly around the facility. Inside each hoop or beside each marker, place colored task cards.

On signal, students begin an activity by moving randomly around the facility.

On the stop signal, students move to the nearest task card and perform the listed activity for 15 seconds.

After completing that activity, they begin a selected fitness activity for 30 seconds, stop on signal, and perform a different challenge.

Teaching Idea: Sample Activities:

Pink: Touch your elbow to the floor, then hop on your right foot ten times, then hop on your left foot ten times.

Green: Touch your right knee to the floor, and then do 15 curl-ups or modified curl-ups.

Yellow: Sit down and stand up 20 times.

Orange: Put your hands on the floor and do 15 "Frisky Pony Kicks".

Gray: Make a bridge and wave to four friends with your right hand, shake your left foot in the air five times, and then wave to four different friends.

White: Jump back and forth over a line 20 times.

Exercise Lines

Focus/Skill: General fitness and coordination.

Procedure/Play: Divide students into three groups: upper body strength, cardiovascular endurance and abdominal strength. Have each group form a line with students approximately arms' distance apart. Assign each group a specific exercise to do within the specified time limit.

All group members for the time limit perform exercises.

After the time limit has expired, students stand, jog for 30 seconds, and come back to their line and prepare for the next exercise.

After completing all exercises, students jog for 30 seconds and walk for another 30 seconds.

Teaching Ideas: Determine the number of repetitions and exercise activities based on the ability and fitness levels of students.

Sample Activities:

1. Upper Body strength: Duration 30 seconds. From push-up position move one hand at a time back and forth over a line as fast as possible. Keep knees off the ground and back straight.

Cardiovascular Endurance: Duration 30 seconds. Keeping feet together jump forward and back as many times as possible. Try jumping side to side.

Abdominal Strength: Duration 30 seconds. Do line beanbag curl-ups: Sit up as far as you can; hold the up position and pass a beanbag under your leg to the person on your right. After passing the beanbag, keep "curling-up" as many times as you can. When the beanbag reaches the end of the line, start passing it back.

Keep Moving

Focus/Skill: General fitness development
Description: student's walk/jog in a circle formation at the center of the facility. Select one student to move to the center and become the leader. When the leader goes to the center, all students stop moving forward, turn to the center, and keep waking in place.

The center leader keeps his or her feet moving and performs any movement as long as the feet keep moving. The students in the circle perform the same movements as the leader.

After 15 seconds, the leader goes back to the circle and all students begin the walk/jog.

After 15 seconds of the walk/jog, a new leader is picked to go to the center and begin his or her movements.

Teaching Idea: Keep students moving rapidly and encourage innovative movements from all leaders. Keep the group going until all students have had the opportunity to be leaders. You may have to shorten the time involved for each leader.

Laterality Fitness

Focus/Skill: Fitness and coordination skills, general fitness development.

Procedure/Play: Space students randomly around the facility. After demonstrating the exercise/activity, have students follow (leader) through the progression.

Teaching Idea Exercises:

1. Random hopping around the room (a hop is on both feet).

Angels in the snow: Go slowly at first, placing emphasis on moving both arms and legs at the same time. More skilled students do jumping jacks.

Arm movements: move both arms at the same time. Lift up, put to the side, small circles, large circles, to the front, down, up high, forward, up etc.

Knee Push-Ups: Use proper form by extending the body forward.

If a student has trouble doing a push-up, have him or he hold a position halfway sown for a few seconds, then go back up.

Stand and Stretch: Reach as high up in the air as possible and hold the position. Go up on toes and balance.

Side leg lifts: Lying on their side with the hand supporting the head, have the students lifted their top leg up and down. Hold the "up" position for approximately five to ten seconds. Roll over and repeat with other leg.

Coffee grinder: from a side-lean position, supporting the body with either the right or left arm and the same foot, have the student move in a circle around the supporting arm 17.

Fitness Dice

Focus/Skill: General fitness development.
Equipment: 1 set of fitness dice per group.
Procedure/Play: The class is divided into small groups. Each group will get one set of fitness dice. Students in each group take a turn in throwing the dice on the floor. The numbered die will be added up and then the exercise die looked at. The children are to perform the exercise that is seen on the dice as well as the number of times. The next person takes a turn; continue until everyone has a chance to go.
Teaching Idea: Children should be encouraged to take turns.

Builders and Bulldozers

Focus/Skill: cardiovascular endurance, agility, and general fitness development.
Equipment: 15-20 cones, pinnies.
Procedure/Play: Cones are spread out over the playing area. Students are divided into builders and bulldozers. The bulldozers are to knock over the cones, and the builders are to immediately go around and set them back up. The students play for approximately five minutes at a time, and then stop to count the cones that are

upright (builders) and count the ones that are knocked down (bulldozers). The players switch roles and repeat.

Teaching Suggestions: In order so that the children are able to determine which are builders/bulldozers, use pinnies to designate. Also remind students to watch where they are going.

Physical Fitness Testing Presidents Challenge Fitness Program

Focus/Skill: General fitness testing.
Procedure/Play:

Curl-Ups. Have students lie down with knees flexed about 12 inches from buttocks. Partner holds feet. Arms are crossed with hands placed on opposite shoulders and elbows held close to chest. Keeping this arm position, student raises the trunk curling up to touch elbows to thighs and then lowers the back to the floor, for one curl-up. Students are timed for one minute.

Shuttle Run. Mark two parallel lines 30 feet apart and place two blocks of wood or similar object behind one of the lines. Students start behind opposite line. To start the student runs to the blocks, picks one up, runs back to the starting line, places block behind the line, runs back and picks up the second block, and runs back across starting line.

Endurance Run/Walk. Students walk a distance of one- mile. Walking may be mixed with running. However, the students should be encouraged to cover the distance in as short a time as possible.

Pull-Ups. Students hangs from a horizontal bar with arms, fully extended and feet free from floor, using either an overhand grasp (palms facing away from body) or underhand grip (palms facing toward body). Small students may be lifted to starting position. Student raises body until chin clears the bar and then lowers body to full-hang starting position. Students perform as many correct pull-ups as possible.

Right Angle Push-Ups. The student lies face down on the mat in push-up position with hands under shoulders, fingers straight, and legs straight, parallel, and slightly apart, with the toes supporting the feet. The student straightens the arms, keeping the back and knees straight, then lowers the body until there is a 90 degree angle at the elbows, with the upper arms parallel to the floor. A partner holds her/ his hand at the point of the 90 degree angle so that the student being tested goes down only until her/his shoulder touches the partner hand, then back up. The push-ups are continued until the student can do no more.

Flexed-Arm Hang. This is an alternate to pull-ups or right-angle push-ups for students who cannot do one pull-up. Using an overhand grasp or underhand grip, student assumes flexed-arm hang position with chin clearing the bar. Students may be lifted to this position. Student holds this position as long as possible.

V-Sit Reach. A straight line two feet long is marked on the floor as the baseline. A measuring line is drawn perpendicular to the midpoint of the baseline extending two feet on each side and marked off in half-inches. The point where the baseline and measuring line intersect is the "0" point. Student removes shoes and sits on floor with measuring line between legs and soles on floor with measuring line between legs and soles of feet placed immediately behind baseline, heels 8-12 inches apart. Students clasps thumbs so that hands are together, palms down, and places them on measuring line. With the legs held flat by a partner, keeping fingers on baseline and feet flexed. After three practice tries, the student holds the fourth reach for three seconds while that distance is recorded.

Sit and Reach. A specially constructed box with a measuring scale marked in centimeters, with 23 centimeters at the level of the feet. Student removes shoes and sits on floor with knees fully extended, feet shoulder-width apart and soles of the feet held flat against the end of the box. With hands on top of each other, palms down, and legs held flat, student reaches along the measuring line as far as possible. After three reaches, the fourth reach is held while the distance is recorded.

Stunts

The developmental level program relies on simple stunts. Stunts requiring exceptional body control, critical balancing, or substantial strength should be left for higher levels of development.

Balance Stunts

One-Leg Balance

Focus/Skill: balance, coordination.

Procedure/Play: Lift one leg from the floor, bring the knee up. The arms should be free at first and then assume specified positions: folded across the chest, on the hips, on the head, or behind the back.

Double-Knee Balance

Focus/Skill: balance, coordination.

Procedure/Play: Kneel on both knees, with the feet pointed to the rear. Lift the feet from the ground and balance on the knees. Vary the position of the arms.

Teaching Suggestions: Experiment with different arm positions.

One-Leg Balance Stunt

Focus/Skill: balance, fundamental concepts of right and left.

Procedure/Play: Each of the following stands should be done with different arms positions, starting with the arms out to the sides and then folded across the chest. Have the children devise other arm positions. Each stunt can be held first for three seconds and then for five seconds. Later, the eyes can be closed during the count. The student should recover to original position with out loss of balance or excessive movement.

Kimbo Stand. With the left foot kept flat on the ground, cross the right leg over the left to a position in which the right foot is pointed partially down and the toe is touching the ground.

Knee-Lift Stand. From a standing position, lift one knee up so that the thigh is parallel to the ground and the toe is pointed down. Hold. Return to starting position.

Stork Stand. From a standing position, shift all of the weight to one foot. Place the other foot so that the sole is against the inside of the knee and thigh of the standing leg. Hold. Recover to standing position.
Teaching Idea: Stunts should be repeated, using the other leg.

Balance Touch
Focus/Skill: balance, fundamental concepts of backward, sideward.
Equipment: beanbags or erasers.
Procedure/Play: Place an object (beanbag, eraser) a yard away from a line. Balancing on one foot, reach out with the other foot, touch the object (no weight should be placed on it) and recover to the starting position. Reach sideward, backward.
Teaching Idea: Try placing the object at various distances. On a gymnasium floor, count the number of boards to establish the distance for the touch.

Single-Leg Balances

Focus/Skill: fundamental concept of forward, backward, right, left.

1. Forward Balance. Extend one leg backward until it is parallel to the floor. Keeping the eyes forward and the arms out to the sides, bend forward, balancing on the other leg. Hold for five seconds without moving. Reverse legs. This is also called a forward scale.

Backward Balance. With knee straight, extend one leg forward, with toes pointed. Keep the arms out to the sides for balance. Lean back as far as possible. The bend should be far enough back so that the eyes are looking at the ceiling.

Side Balance. Stand on the left foot with enough side bends to the left so that the right (top) side of the body is parallel to the floor. Put the right arm alongside the head and in line with the rest of the body. Reverse, using the right leg for support. (Support may be needed momentarily to get into position).

Individual Stunts
Directional Walk
Focus/Skill: Concepts of right and left, balance.
Procedure/Play: For a left movement, begin in standing position. Do all of the following simultaneously: take a step to the left, raise the left arm and point left, turn the head to the left, and state crisply "Left". Close with the right foot back to standing position. Take several steps left and then reverse.

Teaching Idea: Definite and forceful simultaneous movements of the arm head (turn), and leg (step) coupled with a crisp enunciation of the direction are the ingredients of this stunt.

Cross-Legged Stand

Focus/Skill: fundamental concept of right, left.
Procedure/Play: Sit with the legs crossed and the body bent partially forward. Respond approximately to these six commands:
"Touch the right foot with the right hand".
"Touch the left foot with the right hand".
"Touch the right foot with the left hand".
"Touch the left foot with the left hand'.
"Touch both feet with the hands."
"Touch the feet with crossed hands."

The command should be given in varied sequences. The child must interpret that his right foot is on the left side, and vice versa. If this seems too difficult, have the children start with the feet in normal position (uncrossed).

Teaching Idea: Do the stunt with a partner, one child giving the commands and the other responding as directed.

Heel Click

Focus/Skill: balance, coordination, right, left concept.

Procedure/Play: Stand with the feet slightly apart, jump up, and click the heels, coming down with the feet apart. Try with a quarter turn right and left.

Teaching Suggestions:

1. Clap the hands overhead as the heels are clicked.

Join hands with one or more children. Count, "One, two, THREE," jumping on the third count.

Begin with a cross-step to the side, and then click the heels. Try both and left.

Try to click heels twice before landing. Land with the feet apart.

Partner and Group Stunts

Seesaw

Focus/Skill: fundamental concept of up and down.

Procedure/Play: Face and join hands with a partner. Move the seesaw up and down, one child stooping while the other rises. Recite the words to this version of 'Seesaw",

Seesaw, Seesaw
This is how we Seesaw
Seesaw, Seesaw

Teaching Idea: Jump upward at the end of the rise each time.

Double Top

Focus/Skill: balance, coordination, and concept of right and left.

Procedure/Play: Face partner and join hands. Experiment to see which type of grip works best. With straight arms, lean away from each and at the same time move the toes close to partner's. Spin around slowly in either direction, taking tiny steps. Increase speed. Teaching Idea: Use a stooped position. Instead of holding hands, hold a wand and increase the body lean backward. Try the stunt standing right side to right side.

Lead-Up Games for Sports

Softball

The First One Home

Focus/Skill: Batting, retrieving balls, baserunning.
Equipment: plastic bat; whiffle ball, batting tee, 1 set of bases with home plate.
Procedure/Play: a home plate is needed, and a batting tee can use. Foul lines should be marked wide enough so as not to be restrictive. The batter gets as many pitches (or swings) as needed to hit a fair ball. The teacher is the pitcher. The pitches are easy (as in slow-pitch softball), so that the batter has a good chance to hit the ball. The batter hits the ball and runs to first base and back home before the ball is returned to the pitcher. (A marker should designate the pitcher's mound). Other students are used as fielders.
Teaching Idea: A rotation system should be used so that all students have a turn. Also a batting tee can be used. As the students begin to understand the concept of base running, the game may be expanded by having the students hit the ball and run to second base and back, third base and back, etc.

Ball Drop

Focus/Skill: batting, base running.
Equipment: Batting tee, whiffle ball, bucket.
Procedure/Play: Students are divided up into two groups. The teacher is the pitcher, and the students are the fielders. The students

from the first group come up to bat one at a time. The student hitting the ball must place the bat in the bucket before starting to run to first base. This emphasizes the importance of not throwing the bat after hitting the ball.

Teaching Idea: Draw a square on the ground where the bat should be placed if a bucket is not available.

Basketball

Bounce With Me

Focus/Skill: Basic ball handling skills, dribbling, passing, catching.

Equipment: Mini basketballs, playground balls.

Procedure/Play: Give each student an appropriate size ball mini basketball or playground ball. After students have a ball spread them out throughout the facility. Students are directed to perform the following tasks' Can you?

Bounce the ball and catch.

Bounce the ball with right hand while remaining in one place.

Bounce the ball with left hand while remaining in one place.

Bounce pass to a partner-using one hand.

Bounce pass to a partner –using both hands.

Teaching Idea: Modify all activities so that the students are successful, such as using a low basket five to six feet in height, when shooting the ball. Also, be sure to emphasize fundamentals - elbows in, knees slightly bent, push up with a good release and follow-through.

Dribble Basketball

Focus/Skill: dribbling, ball control.

Equipment: mini-basketballs or playground balls.

Procedure/Play: Children are divided into groups with each group in circle formation. A basketball or playground ball is placed in the center of each circle. The students are numbered consecutively in each circle-team. The teacher calls out a number, players in each circle that has that number run to the center, pick up the ball, dribble it out the vacated spot, around the circle, back into the open spot, and into the center of the circle, where they place the ball on the floor. The game resumes by the teacher calling a new number, and continues until all have been called.

Soccer

Soccer Relay

Focus/Skill: trapping, kicking.
Equipment: "12' beach ball
Procedure/Play: Students are divided into groups of four to five and are placed in lanes. On command, a student from each group kicks beach ball (using instep of foot) to the cone on opposite end of court, turn and come back. Continue until all players have gone.

Teaching Idea: Emphasize control and have students perform repetitions enough times to get the maximum use of the activity.

Line Soccer

Focus/Skill: trapping, kicking.
Equipment: "3" soccer ball or playground ball, 2 goals.
Procedure/Play: The students are divided into two groups and the player in each group is given a number. The groups sit on each side of the playing area. A goal area is designated on each end. In the middle of the playing area soccer balls are placed, one for each group. The teacher call out a number from each group, players come out from their respective end, go to center attempt to kick their ball into goal or area that has been designated as goal area. Players retrieve ball and place back in center and go back to seat. Continue until all have gone.

Teaching Idea: Younger children may have difficulty remembering numbers; try alphabet or using their names.

Volleyball

Newcomb
Equipment: 1 trainer volleyball per group.
Focus/Skill: basic volleyball skills.
Procedure/Play: This game is used to teach the concept of volleyball. Students are arranged in volleyball formation, (three on the front row, three on the back). The object is to throw the ball to a teammate, each throw counts as a hit, on the third throw that person that catches the volleyball has to toss it over the net to the other side who in turn attempts to throw it three times to each other and then over. If while attempting to throw it to another person and that person does not make the catch but drops the ball, then the ball goes to the other side.

Hockey

Hockey Dribble

Focus/Skill: gripping, striking.
Equipment: hockey sticks with foam heads, rubber ball.
Procedure/Play: The class is divided into two teams. Each player drives the ball to the cone runs down and retrieves the ball and dribbles back. When the first person in each line gets back, the next person goes until all have been.
Teaching Idea: Have each student dribble to the cone, pick the ball up and jog back.
Developmental Activities 3-5

Apparatus Activities

Activities with Parachutes

* Parachutes are available in various sizes. The parachute should be a size that can be easily handled by children. The parachute

activities should be performed to get the maximum benefits of exercise.

Circular Dribble

Focus/Skill: gripping, overhand and underhand, strength development.

Equipment: parachute, balls for dribbling.

Procedure/Play: Each child has a ball suitable for dribbling. The object is to run in a circular manner counterclockwise, holding onto the parachute with the left hand and dribbling with the right hand, retaining control of the ball. In order to accommodate the left-handed students, try dribbling clockwise. The dribbler should start first, and then on signal, children start to run. If a child loses his ball, he must recover it and try to hook on at his original place.

Teaching Idea: If there is not enough equipment for every child to have a ball, modify the activity by allowing maybe two to three students at a time to dribble, rotating until all have had a chance to dribble.

Numbers

Focus/Skill: gripping, coordination, and agility.

Equipment: Parachute

Procedure/Play: The children are given a number from 1-5. The parachute is raised and a number is called. Those with that number called go into the center and come out at their own places when the center of the parachute starts to come down.

Teaching Idea: Have students perform locomotor skills, stunts, while under the parachute.

Change Numbers

Focus/Skill: Agility, coordination, gripping.

Equipment: Parachute

Procedure/play: The students are numbered off by fours or fives. The children whose number is called move under the parachute, changing places with someone as they come out as the parachute comes down.

Teaching Idea: Encourage safety by reminding students to move carefully under the parachute while trying to find their places.

Steal the Bacon

Equipment: parachute, beanbags or erasers.
Focus/Skill: agility, coordination.
Procedure/Play: The students are divided into groups. A number of objects are placed
under the parachute. When a group is called, they attempt to go under the parachute andattempt to retrieve the bacon before the parachute comes down.

Teaching Idea: Place more than one object under the parachute and have theStudents' retrieve as many as possible before the parachute comes down.

Under the Big Top

Equipment: parachute.
Focus/Skill: speed, agility, and coordination.
Procedure/Play: Students are divided into two groups. One group is holding theparachute and the other group are jogging in place on the outside of the parachute. Onsignal, the group on the outside runs into the middle of the parachute and out again, trying not to get caught as the group holding the parachute attempts to catch them inside as they bring the parachute down.

Parachute Tug-of-War

Focus/Skill: gripping, strength development, and agility.
Equipment: parachute.
Procedure/Play: A line is marked under the parachute. Each team tries to pull the other half of the parachute over the designated line.

Teaching Idea: Have children stand with their backs to the parachute gripping the parachute with both hands, palm down.

Ball Kick

Focus/Skill: coordination, agility.

Equipment: gator skin or any soft balls for kicking,

Procedure/Play: Holding the parachute at waist height, kick several balls underneathback and forth, trying to keep the balls under the parachute.

Teaching Suggestion: Divide the class into groups and try to kick the most balls under.

Activities With Gymnasium Scooters

In order to maintain a safe environment, students should be reminded of scooter safety rules.

Scooter Kick

Equipment: scooters, balls suitable for kicking.

Focus/Skill: gripping, striking, and kicking.

Procedure/Play: Students will be split into two groups, each on one half of the gym. Each child will receive a scooter. Place several balls on the floor. The idea is to by kicking only, get all of the balls on your opponent's side of the playing area. No hands may be used. For safety, students should not be allowed to get off their scooters.

Scooter Kickball

Focus/Skill: striking with various body parts.

Equipment: cage ball, scooters.

Procedure/Play: Divide class into two groups with a student on each end acting as a goalie. The object of the game is to kick the cage ball over the goal line that is defended by the other group. The game starts with a face-off of two opposing players on scooters at the center of the court. Face-off is also used after a goal is scored. Players propel the ball mainly with their feet.

Safety – defenders should be reminded to remain on scooters at all times.

Scooter Bowling

Focus/skill: Maneuvering on a scooter.

Equipment: Six bowling pins, cones, scooters, playground balls.

Procedure: Divide the players into two teams, at the end of each line six pins are placed. A penalty line is needed (floor tape) to keep the players from staying too close to the pins. The players, sitting on scooters and holding a ball spread out on their end of the playing area. On command, the players roll their ball attempting to knock down opponent's pins. The object is to get as many opponents balls on their side, and to knock down all opponents' pins.

Teaching Idea: increase the number of pins on each side.

Scooter Hula Hoop

Focus/Skill: tagging, pulling, and maneuvering.

Equipment: scooters, pinnies for teams, whiffle balls, tennis balls, and erasers.

Procedure/Play: Divide the class into four teams. Place a hoop at the other end of the playing area. Each hoop contains items of beanbag; whiffle ball, tennis ball, and erasers. The first player on each team maneuvers to hoop, take an item out of his/her hoop and rolls back to the line on the scooter, tags the next person in line who rolls on scooter to retrieve the next item and returns on scooter to tag the next person and so on. Continue this until everyone in each line has gone. Time the game to see how long it takes for each team to finish.

Safety statement: all players move in the same direction and watch where they are going.

Scooter Tag

Focus/Skill: tagging, pulling, and maneuvering.
Equipment: pinnies for one team, scooters.
Procedure: On command one team will start chasing the other team on scooters. Any players going out of bounds, falling off scooters or getting tagged receives one point (rather than eliminating). If one player is tagged by another who is falling off their scooter it does not count. After five minutes scores are given and teams switch.
Teaching Idea: Play with four teams instead of two.

Scooter Basketball

Focus/Skill: striking, pulling, maneuvering.
Equipment: scooters, 1 "12" inch Gator Skin ball, 2 milk crates or boxes.
Procedure/Play: Divide the class into two teams facing each other. Give each person on each team a number. Place the scooters in front of students; call out two numbers from each team. Those students come out and get on scooter and roll the ball that is placed in the center of playing area. First person that gets to the ball passes to teammate and they attempt to get close enough to drop ball into goal (which is a crate or box). Players are guarded just like in basketball except they cannot get off their scooters. A boundary line is placed in front of each crate; the defense cannot go over this line. (This prevents crowding at the basket). Continue until all have gone.
Teaching Idea: Use four players instead of two.
Safety Statement: Students should be careful when rolling on scooters.

Scoop It Up

Focus/Skill: maneuvering, striking, and pulling.
Equipment: scooters, scoops and whiffle balls.
Procedure/Play: Groups are divided into four teams. The playing area is divided into halves with two teams on each half. Each team has 1 offensive, 1 defensive player. Players number off. Call one number from each team. One team puts the ball into play. Players on offense may go anywhere on the court. Players on defense have to stay back and protect (goal) hoop. Player on defense starts the game by attempting to pass the ball to the offensive player who attempts to throw the ball through the opponents hoop. Any player who misses a shot and gets their own rebound must pass to a teammate before another shot is attempted. Players may receive penalty shot if players foul them while in the act of shooting. Direct free throws is given to opponents any time a player uses their hand to pick up a ball or gets off their scooter. Switch after three or minutes of play until all have gone on offense and defense.
Teaching Idea: Players are reminded to use a snap throw (using mostly the wrist) when using the scoop.

Scooter Volleyball

Focus/Skill: setting, bumping, maneuvering, and pulling.
Equipment: scooters, volleyball net, trainer VB.
Procedure/Play: Two teams, sitting on a scooter face each other on opposite sides of the net. The game is played to 15, even if it is tied at 14 points. One team starts the game with a serve, which can be thrown or hit over the net while on the scooter. Game is played like Volleyball only on the scooters. The back line players must not pass the front line players to hit the ball. Players cannot hit the ball twice in a row, fall off their scooter while holding the ball or holds the ball for more than three seconds.
Teaching Idea: Remind players that when serving to keep the ball slightly to one side.

Row Your Boat

Focus/Skill: pulling, pushing.

Equipment: scooters, cones

Procedure/Play: the class is separated into four teams; the teams are in file formation. On command, he first player from each team sitting in his/her scooter and using the cone, will pull to the opposite end push him/herself back. The next in line may leave when the player in front has reached the opposite sideline. Continue until every student has had a turn. The players may not use their hands to touch other players, or touch the floor. The cones must be held in an upright position.

Teaching Idea: Have two players go at the same time, with one student pulling and the other one pushing. Both players have to keep their hands on the cone.

Safety Statement: Remind students not to throw the cones or overextend themselves when placing the cone. The scooter could tip over causing injury.

Bombs Away

Focus/Skill: rolling, maneuvering.

Equipment: playground balls, scooters, and pinnies.

Procedure/Play: Facing each other are two teams are facing each other. Designate two players from each team to be medics. Players are sitting on scooters they may move anywhere on their own side of the court. If a player or scooter is hit with a rolling ball, that player has to sit by his/her scooter. The medics may rescue them by placing placing them on medic scooter and pulling them to their own end line. Players are temporarily out of the game if they go past the half-court to retrieve a ball or fall of a scooter to avoid getting hit. Players may remain in the game if they are hit with a thrown or bouncing ball. Medics may be rescued only by another medic.

Teaching Idea: Remind players to keep hands out from under the scooters.

Physical Fitness Activities

A good, sound fitness program is essential in the development of children. It is important that students understand the need to be physically active early in life and to maintain a level of fitness throughout adulthood.

Circle Race

Focus/Skill: running, tagging, coordination, and agility.

Procedure/Play: children are arranged in a circle numbered off by threes. When the teacher calls that number, the student who has been assigned that number leave their places, run around the circle once, and back to the place, trying to tag as many children in front of them as possible.

Teaching Idea: Encourage running as close to the circle as possible and having controlled tags and stops. Also to decrease the number of children running around the circle, instead of numbering off by threes give each from each circle student a number.

Color Tag

Focus/Skill: balance, speed, stopping, starting.

Equipment: colored hoops, squares or circles in at least 3 or 4 colors.

Procedure/Play: Students are divided into color groups of equal size. Colored hoops or spot markers for each color group are scattered throughout the playing area, numbering one less than the number of children in each group. One person from each group is designated as "IT". The children of each color group attempt to move from one square to another while "IT" tries to tag them. The children are safe when they are touching the square or are in the hoop of their color only. "IT" may tag only those in the same color group. "IT" changes position with the child tagged.

Teaching Idea: Students should look out for others as the move throughout the playing area and tagging softly.

Indy 500

Focus/Skill: running, tagging, cardiovascular endurance.

Procedure/Play: The students start in a large circle and are numbered off in threes or fours. The game begins by teacher calling out a number and those children with the corresponding number run clockwise around the circle and try to tag players in front of them. On command, all runners have to stop and return to their original position. Continue to call out numbers until all players have gone.

Teaching Idea: On signal have all runners change direction and proceed counter clockwise. Encourage safety, and change the starter often.

Car Lot

Focus/Skill: running, tagging, agility.

Equipment: Pinnies or vests of 4 different colors

Procedure/Play: One player is "it" and stands in the center of the playing area between two lines that are approximately 50 feet apart. The class selects four brands of cars (Honda, Corvette, etc.). Each student then selects a car from the four but does not tell anyone what it is. The class is then divided into the car groups by colors. The teacher calls out a car name, all students who selected that name attempt to run to the other side without getting tagged. The teacher calls out the cars until all students have run. When the teacher calls out "Car Lot" all of the cars must go. The game is played until all students have been tagged.

Flag Chase

Focus/Skill: running, tagging, cardiovascular endurance

Equipment: Flags

Procedure/Play: One team wears flags positioned in the back of the belt. The flag team scatter through out the area. On signal, the object is for the chasing team to capture as many flags as possible in a designated amount of time. The flags are brought to the teacher or placed in a box. Players cannot use their hands to ward off a chaser. Roles are then reversed. Players continue until all opponents' flags are pulled.

PacMan

Focus/Skill: running, tagging, agility
Equipment: Pinnies
Procedure/Play: Designate three students to be "it by wearing a pinnie. The remainder of the class is scattered throughout the area standing on a floor line. Movement can only be made on a line. Begin the game by placing the three taggers at the corners of the perimeter lines. Play is continued; a player who is tagged takes the pinnie and becomes the new tagger. If a player leaves a line to escape being tagged, that player has to take a pinnie and become a tagger.

Physical Fitness Testing President's Challenge Program[14]

Focus/Skill: General fitness testing.
Procedure/Play:

1. Curl-Ups. Have students lie down with knees flexed about 12 inches from buttocks. Partner holds feet. Arms are crossed with hands placed on opposite shoulders and elbows held close to chest. Keeping this arm position, student raises the trunk curling up to touch elbows to thighs and then lowers the back to the floor, for one curl-up. Students are timed for one minute.
2. Shuttle Run. Mark two parallel lines 30 feet apart and place two blocks of wood or similar object behind one of the lines. Students start behind opposite line. To start the student runs to the blocks, picks one up, runs back to the starting line, places block behind the line, runs back and picks up the second block, and runs back across starting line.

3. Endurance Run/Walk. Students walk a distance of one- mile. Walking may be mixed with running. However, the students should be encouraged to cover the distance in as short a time as possible.

4. Pull-Ups. Students hangs from a horizontal bar with arms, fully extended and feet free from floor, using either an overhand grasp (palms facing away from body) or underhand grip (palms facing toward body). Small students may be lifted to starting position. Student raises body until chin clears the bar and then lowers body to full-hang starting position. Students perform as many correct pull-ups as possible.

5. Right Angle Push-Ups. The student lies face down on the mat in push-up position with hands under shoulders, fingers straight, and legs straight, parallel, and slightly apart, with the toes supporting the feet. The student straightens the arms, keeping the back and knees straight, then lowers the body until there is a 90 degree angle at the elbows, with the upper arms parallel to the floor. A partner holds her/his hand at the point of the 90 degree angle so that the student being tested goes down only until her/his shoulder touches the partner hand, then back up. The push-ups are continued until the student can do no more.

Flexed-Arm Hang. This is an alternate to pull-ups or right-angle push-ups for students who can not do one pull-up. Using an overhand grasp or underhand grip, student assumes flexed-arm hang position with chin clearing the bar. Students may be lifted to this position. Student holds this position as long as possible.

V-Sit Reach. A straight line two feet long is marked on the floor as the baseline. A measuring line is drawn perpendicular tot he midpoint of the baseline extending two feet on each side and marked off in half-inches. The point where the baseline and measuring line intersect is the "0" point. Student removes shoes and sits on floor with measuring line between legs and soles on floor with measuring line between legs and soles of feet placed immediately behind baseline, heels 8-12 inches apart. Students clasps thumbs so that hands are together, palms down, and places them on measuring line. With the legs held flat by a partner, keeping fingers on baseline and feet flexed. After three practice tries, the student holds the fourth reach for three seconds while that distance is recorded.

Sit and Reach. A specially constructed box with a measuring scale marked in centimeters, with 23 centimeters at the level of the feet. Student removes shoes and sits on floor with knees fully extended, feet shoulder-width apart and soles of the feet held flat against the end of the box. With hands on top of each other, palms down, and legs held flat, student reaches along the measuring line as far as possible. After three reaches, the fourth reach is held while the distance is recorded.

Stunts

Normal introductory activities and fitness development activities usually supply sufficient warm-up for the stunt lesson.

Toe Jump

Hold the left toe with the right hand. Jump the right foot through without losing the grip on the toes. Try with the other foot.

Front Seat Support

Sit on the floor with the legs together and forward. Place the hands flat on the floor, somewhat between the hips and the knees with fingers pointed forward. Push down so the hips come off the floor with the weight supported on the hands and heels. Next lift the heels and support the entire weight of the body on the hands for three to five seconds.

Individual Stunts

Skiers Sit

Assume a sitting position against a wall with the thighs parallel to the floor and the knees joints at right angles. (The position is the same as sitting in a chair, but of course there is no chair). The arms are held in front of the chest. The feet should be flat on the floor and the lower legs straight up and down. Try to sit for 30 seconds, 45 seconds, and 1 minute.

Teaching Idea: Support the body with crossed legs.

Heel Click (Side)

Balance on one foot, with the other out to the side. Hop on the supporting foot; click the heels and return to balance. Try with the other foot. The student should recover to the one-foot balance position without excessive foot movement.

JackKnife

Stand erect with the hands out to the front and a little to the side. Jump up and bring the feet up quickly to touch the hands. Vary by starting with a short run. Be sure the feet come up to the hands rather than the hands moving down to the feet. Do several jackknife in succession. The takeoff must be with both feet and good height must be achieved.

Heel and Toe Spring

Place the heels against a line. Jump backward over the line while bent over and grasping the toes. (Lean forward slightly to allow for impetus and then jump backward over the line). Try jumping forward to the original position. To be successful, the child should retain the grasp on the toes. The teacher can introduce the stunt by first having the children grasp their ankles when making the jump.

Single Leg Circle (Pinwheel)

Assume a squatting position with both hands on the floor, left knee between the arms and right leg extended to the side. Swing the right leg forward and under the lifted right arm, under the left arm and back to the starting position. Several circles should be made in succession. Reverse the position and try with the left leg.

Tandem Bicycle

One child forms a bicycle position, with the back against a wall and knees bent as if sitting. The feet should be placed under the body. The second child backs up and sits down lightly on the first child's knees. Other children may be added in the same fashion, their hands around the waist of the player immediately in front for support. Forward progress is made by moving the feet on the same side together.

Wheel Barrow

One child gets down on the hands with feet extended to the rear and legs apart. The other partner (the pusher) grasps partners' legs about halfway between the ankles and knees. The wheelbarrow walks forward on the hands, supported by the pusher. Movements should be under control. Students tend to grasp the legs too near the feet. The pusher must not push too fast. The wheelbarrow should have the head up and look forward. Fingers should be pointed forward and well spread, with the pads of the fingers supporting much of the weight. The pusher should carry the legs low and keep the arms extended.

Partner Rising Sun

Partners lie facedown on the floor with heads together and feet in opposite directions. They hold volleyball or some ball similar size,

70

between their heads. Working together, they stand up and return to position while retaining control of the ball. Do not touch the ball with the hands. A slightly deflated ball works best. Some caution is necessary to prevent bumping heads if ball is suddenly squeezed out.

Lead Up Games for Sports

Games require a combination of skills. Lead-up games are developed for the express purpose of limiting the number of skills needed for successful participation.

Basketball Tag

Focus/Skill: catching, passing, dribbling, and guarding
Equipment: foam rubber basketball, pinnies.
Procedure/Play: Designate three to five students to be "it "and have them wear a pinnie. The rest of the class passes the ball and tries to tag one of the students who is it with ht ball. If desired more than one ball can be used. Players can move the ball by dribbling or passing to teammates. The player who is it tries to avoid moving near the ball while others try to pass, dribble and move near the roving "it". The team without the ball plays defense and tries to intercept the ball.

Hockey Keep-Away

Focus/Skill: passing, fielding.
Equipment: One hockey stick per student, puc or ball.
Procedure/Play: Players are spread evenly around the circle with one player in the center. The object of the game is to keep the player in the center from touching the puck. The puck is passed back and forth with emphasis on accurate passing and fielding.

If the player in the center touches the puck the player who last passed the puck takes the place of the center player. A change of players also can be made after a passing or fielding error.

Pin Kickball

Focus/Skill: kicking.
Equipment: soccer ball or playground ball.
Procedure/Play: Two teams start about 20 feet apart, facing each other. At least six pins are placed between the two lines of players. One ball is given to each team at the start of kicking. Kicks should be made from the line behind which the team is standing. Players should trap and concentrate on accuracy. Try to see which team can knock down the most pins.
Teaching Idea: The number of pins, balls, and players can be varied easily.

Kick Softball

Focus/Skill: kicking, throwing, catching, running.
Equipment: Soccer ball or playground ball.
Procedure/Play: The batter stands in the kicking area, a 3 feet square home plate. The batter kicks the ball rolled on the ground by the pitcher. The ball should be rolled at a moderate speed. An umpire (teacher) calls balls and strikes. A strike is a ball that rolls over the 3 feet square. A ball is one that rolls outside this area. There are no strikeouts or walks. No base stealing is permitted.
Teaching Idea: Punch Ball. The batter can hit volleyball as in a volleyball serve or punch a ball pitched by the pitcher.

3 and Over

Focus/Skill: catching
Equipment: Volleyball or Trainer Volleyball.
Procedure/Play: The game three and over emphasizes the basic offensive strategy of volleyball. The game follows regular volleyball rules with the exception that the ball must be played 3 times before going over the net. The team loses the serve or the point of the ball s not played three times.

Birdie in the Cage

Focus/Skill: passing, catching, intercepting

Equipment: soccer ball, basketball or volleyball

Procedure/Play: Players are in a circle formation with one child in the middle. The object of the game is for the center player to try to touch the ball. The ball is passed from player in the circle, and the center player attempts to touch the ball. The player who passed the ball that was touched takes their place in the center. In case of a poor pass resulting in the balls leaving the circle area, the player who caused the error now changes to the center of the circle.

Teaching Idea: As few as three children can play, with two children passing the ball back and forth between them while a third tries to touch it.

Five Passes

Focus/Skill: passing, catching, guarding

Equipment: football, pinnies.

Procedure/Play: The class is split into groups of five each. The object of the game is to complete five consecutive passes, which scores a point. The game is started with a jump ball at the free-throw line. The teams observe regular basketball rules in ball handling in regards to traveling and fouling. At least five consecutive passes must be made by a team who count out loud as the passes are completed. The ball must not be passed back to the person from whom it was received. No dribbling is allowed. If for any reason the ball is fumbled and recovered or improperly passed, a new count is started. After a successful score, the ball can be thrown up again in a center jump at the free-throw line. A foul draws a free throw, which can be marked to avoid confusion.

Twenty-One

Focus/Skill: shooting, ball control
Equipment: basketball
Procedure/Play: Players are in file formation, groups of five, depending on class size. The first player in each line has a basketball each player is permitted two shots from anywhere in the lane. Each shot counts as one point. The object is to see how long it takes the entire class to reach 21.
Teaching Idea: Various combinations and types of shots may be used.

Dribble

Focus/Skill: dribbling, protecting the ball.
Equipment: Soccer balls.
Procedure/Play: A playing area is marked off by cones. All players dribble within this area. Each player dribbles a soccer ball throughout the area, controlling the ball so that it does not touch another ball. If a touch occurs, both players go outside the area and dribble counterclockwise around the area. Once they have completed that, they may comeback into the activity.
Teaching Idea: If using small space such as multipurpose room, smaller groups are recommended. Have students go for five to six minutes at a time then rotate. Also use a soft indoor soccer ball for inside.

Tee Ball

Focus/skill: catching, throwing, hitting, and striking.
Equipment: softball, bat, and batting tee.
Procedure/Play: A version of softball played under softball rules. Instead of hitting a pitched ball, the batter hits the ball from a tee. After the batter hits the ball the play is the same as in regular softball. With no pitching, there is no stealing. A runner stays on base until the

ball is hit by the batter. A fielder occupies the position normally held by the pitcher. The primary duty of the fielder is to field bunts and ground balls and to have back up infielders on throws. Have the teams change to the field after each player has had a turn at bat.

Teaching Idea: To ensure batter has good position make sure the tee is adjusted to batters swing.

Mix and Match

Focus/Skill: Fundamental locomotor movements.

Equipment: none

Procedure/Play: A line is established through the middle of the playing area. Half of the students are on one side and half are on the other side. There must be an odd person, the teacher or another child. The teacher gives the signal for the children to move as directed on their side of the line. They can be told to run, hop, skip, etc. At another signal, the children run to the dividing line, and each reaches across to join hands with a child from the opposite group. The goal is to not be left out. Children may reach over but may not cross the line. The person left out is moved to the opposite side so that the players left out come from alternating sides of the area.

Teaching Idea: The game can also be played to music.

Freeze

Focus/Skill: locomotor movement

Equipment: None

Procedure/Play: Students are scattered about the playing area. On command, they move throughout the area by walking, running, jumping or other movement depending on the command. On command to stop, they freeze and do not move. Any child caught moving after the command is given pays a penalty.

Teaching Idea: Specify the level at which the children must freeze.

Fly Trap

Focus/Skill: fundamental locomotor skills.
Equipment: none.
Procedure/Play: The class is divided into two groups. One group is sitting on the floor. This group is called the Trap. The other children are the flies, and they buzz around the seated children. When a whistle is blown the flies must freeze where they are. If any of the trappers can touch a fly, that fly sits down at that spot and becomes a trapper. The trapper must keep their seats glued to the floor. The game continues until all flies have been caught or for an extended period of time.
Teaching Idea: Change locomotion directions, after all flies have been caught group changes direction.

Back to Back

Focus/Skills: fundamental locomotor movements.
Equipment: None.
Procedure/Play: On command each student stands back to back with another child. One child will be without a partner. This student claps the hands for the next signal and all children change partners with the extra player from the previous game seeking a partner.
Teaching Idea: Add an extra command such as skip, hop, jump, and slide.

Squirrel in the Trees

Focus: fundamental locomotor movements.
Equipment: None
Procedure/Play: Have students form trees by two players facing each other and holding hands on each other's shoulders. A squirrel is in the center of each tree, and one or two extra squirrels are outside. A signal to change is given. All squirrels move out of their tree to another tree and the extra players try to find a free tree. Only one squirrel is allowed in a tree.

Teaching Idea: As a system of rotation when each squirrel moves into a tree, he/she can change places with one of the players forming the tree. The rotation is important because it ensures that all children are active.

Red Light

Focus/Skill: fundamental locomotor skills.
Equipment: none.
Procedure/Play: A goal line is established at one end of the area. The object of the game is to move across the area successfully without getting caught. One player is the leader and stands on the goal line. The leader (Teacher) turns away from the players and claps their hands five times and turns around on the fifth clap. In the meantime, the players move toward the goal line, timing their movements to end on the fifth clap. If the leader catches any movement by any player, that person is required to return to the starting line. The leader can turn around any time to catch movement. The first student to reach the goal line without being caught can become the leader for the next game.

Home Base

Focus/Skill: locomotor movements.
Procedure/Play: The area is divided into four quadrants with cones or floor lines. Each quadrant is the home for one of the squads. The captain of the squad wears a pinnie for easy identification. The teams begin in a straight line sitting on the floor. The teacher calls out a locomotor movement, which the players use to move throughout the area. When the teacher calls "Home base," the students return to their quadrant and return to their starting position behind their captain. The object is to be the first team to return to proper position.

Teaching Ideas: Use different formations, which students must assume upon return to their home base.

Follow Me

Focus/Skill: Locomotor movements.
Equipment: A marker for each child (squares of cardboard can be used).
Procedure/Play: Children are arranged in a rough circle, each standing or sitting with one
Foot on their marker. An extra player is the guide. He moves around the circle, pointing at different players asking them to follow. Each player chosen falls in behind the guide. The guide then takes the group on a tour, and the members of the group perform just as the guide does. The guide may hop, skip, or other locomotor movements and the children follow must do the same. At the signal, "Home" all run for places with a marker. This child chooses another guide.
Teaching Ideas: Making the last child the new leader is not good because this may cause some children to lag and try to be last.

Whistle Mixer

Focus/Skill: All basic locomotor movements.
Procedure/Play: Children are scattered throughout the playing area. To start they may walk around in any direction they wish. The teacher blows a whistle a number of times in a row with short, sharp blasts. The children then form small circles with the number in the circles equal to the number of whistle blasts. If there are four blasts, the children form circles of four only. The goal is to not be the one left out or caught in the circle with the incorrect number of students. Students should be encouraged to move to the center of the area and raise their hands to facilitate finding others without a group. After the circles are formed the teacher calls "walk" and the game continues. In walking the children should move in different directions.

Non-Locomotor Skills

*Non-locomotor skills include bending, twisting, turning,

moving toward and away from the center of the body and other body movements done in place.

Marching Points

Focus/Skill: Non-locomotor movements.

Procedure/Play: One student, crouches in the center of the circle formed by other children. Two goal lines on opposite sides of the circle are the safe areas. The children march around the circle in step, counting as they do. On command students in the center jumps up and attempts to tag the others before they can reach the safety area. Anyone tagged joins the person in the center and helps catch the other children the next time. After six to eight children have: been caught a new game begins.

Teaching Idea: Other non-locomotor movements can be tried.

Popcorn

Focus/Skill: bending, twisting, and stretching.

Procedure/Play: The teacher should give an introduction of how popcorn pops in relation to the heat applied. Half of the children are designated as popcorn; they crouch down in the center of the circle formed by the rest of the children. The circle children, also crouching represents the heat. One of them is designated the leader and will act as a guide to the other students. The children in the circle gradually rise to a standing position, extend their arms overhead, and shake them vigorously to indicate heat. In the meantime the popcorn in the center starts to pop. This should begin at a slow pace and increase in speed and height as the heat is applied. After a time the group change places and action is repeated.

Arches

Focus/Skill: marching, bend, twist, raise, and lifting, lower, turn, curl.

79

Procedure/Play: Facing each other, two players form an arch by standing facing each other with hands joined and arms raised. The arch is placed in the playing area. On signal from the teacher, other players move in a circle passing under the arch. On whistle, the arch is brought down by dropping the hands. All students caught in the arch immediately pairs off to form other arches, keeping in a general circle formation. If a caught player does not have a partner, he/she waits in the center of the circle until one is available. The last players caught (or left) form arches for the next game. The arches should be warned not to bring down their hands and arms too forcefully so that the children passing under are not hurt.

Bumper Lift

Focus/Skill: lifting, bending, and pushing.
Equipment: 1 '13'-playground ball for every 4 players.
Procedure/Play: The four players in each group place the bottoms of their feet against the playground ball. On command, all the players in the group attempt to lift their buttocks or "bumpers" off the floor and hold for three seconds. If they are successful, have them go again to see how long this position can be held. The body has to be completely off the floor except for the hands. One player in each group will give the command to lift, and will count the seconds.
Teaching Ideas: Remind the players that it is easier if they bend their knees.

Hoop Croquet

Focus/Skill: crawling, bending, twisting, and stretching.
Equipment: hula-hoops and holders, cones.
Procedure/Play: There are four teams with six players on each team. The first player on each team will run and crawl through the five hoops directly in front of him/her, go around the cone, return and repeat the course. When the first player has passed the far cone, the next player in the line may leave. This procedure is followed for 10

minutes. Any player leaving before the far cone is passed has to return and do it correctly before continuing. Each player finishing will return to the end of the line. Players may bypass a hoop if they pass or tag a runner approaching or going through a hoop. Any hoop knocked down has to be replaced by that player. If a hoop is not replaced before the next runner arrives, that runner may also by pass that hoop.

Chariot Relay

Focus/Skill: Non-locomotor movements.
Procedure/Play: The class is divided into groups of three with two or more teams in file formation. The chariot is formed by two players who grasp each other's hand as they stand side by side. A third player, the driver stands behind the two and grasps the two outside hands of the Chariot pair. The three in this formation move from one end of the playing area and back, after which the next three players form their chariot.

Do This, Do That

Focus/Skill: Non-locomotor movements.
Procedure/Play: A student is chosen to lead the other children in certain designated or spontaneous movements (bend, twist, etc.). As the leader goes through the non-locomotor movements he/she says "Do This", or "Do That". On "Do This", the other children must do as the leader is doing. If the command is "Do That", no one should move, anyone who does move on this command has to sit down in place. The next leader is that child who is the last to remain standing.

Jump the Shot

Focus/Skill: Non-locomotor movements.
Equipment: A jump the shot rope.
Procedure/Play: The player's stand in a circle facing the center.

The player holding the rope kneels in the center of the circle and turns the rope, playing it out to its full length until the momentum keeps the weighted end of it turning under the feet of the players in the circle who must jump over it. Any player who touches the rope with his feet while it is turning leaves the circle. The last player out turns the rope for the next game.

Non-locomotor Tag

Focus/skill: Non-locomotor movements.
Procedure/Play: Players are scattered over the playing area. The child who is "IT" tells the other children how to move. "IT" must do the same movements. The player whom he/she tags becomes" IT".

Loop Touch

Focus/Skill: Non-locomotor movements.
Procedure/Play: Divide the students into pairs. The players are divided into pairs, standing facing each other on the end lines. When the signal is given, the partners run to the center lines, join right hands, run around each other (right-hand loop) and return to their starting line. Without stopping they run to their partners, make the left loop and return. They repeat with the two-hand loop. The repeat with the two-hand loop. Continue until all have gone.

Manipulative Activities k-2

Stop Ball

Focus/Skill: Throwing, catching.
Equipment: playground balls.
Procedure/Play: The students are in circle formation, with one player in the center of the circle. This player has their hands over his/her eyes. A ball is tossed clockwise or counterclockwise from child

to child around the circle. Failing to catch the ball or making a bad toss causes the student to take one long step back and stay out of the game for one turn. When the command to Stop is given, the player caught with the ball steps back and stays out for one turn. The student in the center of the circle is allowed three or four turns before they are changed.

Leader Ball

Focus/Skill: Throwing, catching.
Equipment: Volleyball or rubber playground ball.
Procedure/Play: The teacher is the leader and stands about 10 feet in front of others who are lined up facing the teacher. The object of the game is to move up to the teacher spot by not making any bad throws and by not by missing any catches. The teacher throws to each child in turn, beginning with the child on the left who must catch and return the ball. Any child making a throwing or catching error goes to the end of the line, on the teachers' right. Those in the line may move up, filling the vacated space. If the teacher makes a mistake, he/she must go to the end of the line and the child at the head becomes the new leader.

Teaching Ideas: The teacher can suggest specific methods of throwing, and catching, such as catch with the right hand only, or don't let the ball touch your body.

Tag

Focus/Skill: Throwing, running.
Equipment: beanbag, fleece ball.
Procedure/Play: One student is designated "It" and has a beanbag or fleece ball. The other students are scattered around the playing area. The player with the bag or ball runs after the others and attempts to hit another player with the object. The person hit becomes it, and the game continues. The tagger must throw the ball or bag, not merely touching another person with it. The rules of tagging should be reviewed for safety.

Teaching Idea: Make more than one student "It". Specifiy the kind of throw to be used, (overhand throw, underhand throw).

Bottle Kick Ball

Focus/Skill: kicking
Equipment: bowling, pins, balls suitable for kicking.
Procedure/Play: Players form a large circle around the bowling pins that are in the middle of the circle. Students kick the ball and try to knock over the pins.
Teaching Ideas: Use as many balls as necessary to keep all the children active. If the group is large, make more than circle of players.

Circle Straddle Ball

Focus/Skill: catching, throwing, and rolling.
Equipment: Two or more 8-inch foam balls.
Procedure/Play: Children are in circle formation of 10-15 students each. Each student stands in a wide straddle stance with the side of the foot against the person standing next to him or her. The hands are on the knees two balls are used. The object of the game is to roll one of the balls between the legs of another player before he can get his hands down to stop the ball. Keep all circles small so that students have more opportunities to handle the ball.

Club Guard

Focus/Skill: throwing.
Equipment: Indian club or bowling pins, foam rubber ball, hula-hoop.
Procedure/Play: Children form a circle. The Indian club is put in the center of the circle inside a hula-hoop. A student stands in the middle of the circle to guard the club. The other children stand outside the large circle, which is the restraining line for them. The

circle players throw the ball at the club and try to knock it down. The guard tries to block the throws with the legs and body. They must stay out of the inner circle. The outer circle players pass the ball around so that one of the players can get an opening to throw. Whoever knocks down the club or pin becomes the new guard.

One Step

Focus/Skill: throwing, catching.

Equipment: A ball, beanbag for each pair of students.

Procedure/Play: Approximately three feet apart two students stand facing each other with one of the students holding a ball or beanbag. The object of the game is to throw or toss the item in a manner so that the partner can catch it without moving from his/her spot. When the throw is completed successfully, the thrower takes one step backward and waits for the throw from his/her partner. Children can try to increase their distance to an established line. When either child misses, moves the feet, or fails to follow directions, partners move forward and start over.

Teaching Ideas: To keep activity interesting and challenging vary the type of throw and catch. Throwing can be underhand, overhand, two-handed etc.

Keep It In, Keep It Out

Focus/Skill: Underhand throw.

Equipment: bean bags

Procedure/Play: The students are in a circle formation with one person in the center of the circle. The beanbags are placed in the center of the circle. The circle player attempts to keep the beanbags out of the circle while the remaining players attempt to keep them in with an underhand throw.

Teaching Idea: The game may be modified to have more than one person in the circle if needed. Encourage the students to look for the empty space to put the beanbags to make it more difficult for the players to keep the beanbags out of their area.

Fleece Ball

Focus/Skill: Overhand throw
Equipment: Fleece balls for every 2 children.
Procedure/Play: Half of the children are scattered over the playing area. On command, the children throw the fleece balls into the opposite side of the playing area. They continue to field and throw balls until the signal to stop is given. On the signal to stop have each child with a ball hold it high in the air. Any fleece ball thrown after the signal to stop is given is returned to the side from which they were thrown. The object is to be the team with the fewest balls on your side.

Body Management

*This wide variety of activities in am educational movement lesson offers children a broad spectrum of activity and offers movement that stimulates all children.

Soap Bubbles

Focus/Skill: body management, balance, and coordination.
Equipment: Cones to designate space, music.
Procedure/Play: Each player is a soap bubble floating through out the area. The teacher calls out the locomotor movement that the children use to move in the area. The entire area is used to start the game. As the game progresses the size area is decreased by moving the cones. Bubbles freeze on signal. Music can be used to stimulate movement. The object of the game is to not collide with another bubble. When this happens, bubbles burst and sink to the floor and make themselves small as possible. The space is made smaller until those who are have not been touched are still standing. Those players who are broken bubbles move to an area. This teaches how to move in general space without touching anyone.

Pairs

Focus/Skill: Body management.

Procedure/Play: Students find a space in the playing area. Each student has a partner (twin). The teacher gives a command such as "take three steps and two leaps", or 'walk backward four steps and three skips". When the pairs are separated the teacher says," find your twin", players find their twin and stand frozen back to back. The goal is to not be the last pair to find each other and assume the frozen position. Students need to move away from each other during the movement. Try to find a new twin each time.

Teaching Ideas: The game becomes more challenging when played in groups of three (triplets). When using this variation, new partners should be selected each time.

Statues

Focus/Skill: Body Management, applying force, balance.

Procedure/Play: Students are scattered in pairs around the area. One student is the swinger and the other student is the statue. The teacher issues a command such as 'pretty', "funny", "happy", "angry". The swingman takes the statue gently by one or both hands, swings it around in a small circle two or three times (teacher should specify) and release it. The statue then takes a pose in keeping with the command and the swinger sits down on the floor. Teacher can decide which are appropriate statues. The partners reverse positions. Children should be reminded that the purpose of the swinging is to position the statues and that it must be controlled for safety.

Circle Stoop

Focus/Skill: Moving to the rhythm.

Equipment: Music or drum.

Procedure/Play: Children are in a single circle, facing counterclockwise. A march or similar music such as a drum can be used. The children march with good posture until the music stops. As soon as a child no longer hears the music or boat, he/she stoops and touches both hands to the ground without losing his/her balance. The last child to touch both hands to the ground and those children who lost balance pay a penalty by going into the center of the circle and waiting out the next round of the game. The children march in good posture, and anyone stooping, even partially, before the music stops should be penalized. The duration of the music should be varied.

Teaching Idea: Using music, have the children employ different locomotor movements such as skipping, hopping and galloping.

Change Sides

Focus/Skill: Body management.
Procedure/Play: Two parallel lines are established 30 feet apart. Half of the children are on each line. On command, all students cross to the other line, face the center, and stand at attention. The objective is to be the first group to do this activity correctly. Children are reminded to be careful when passing through the opposite group. They should be spaced well along each line. This allows room for them to move through each group. The locomotor movements should be varied.

Right Angle

Focus/Skill: Body management
Equipment: Music
Procedure/Play: A drum can be used to provide rhythm for this activity. Some of the basic rhythm records can be used to do this activity. The children change direction at right angles on each heavy beat or change of music. The object of the game is to make the right-angle change on signal and not to bump into other players.

Whistle March

Focus/Skill: Balance, coordination.

Equipment: Music

Procedure/Play: Music with a brisk march should be used. The students are scattered around the room, individually walking in various directions and keeping time to music. A whistle is blown a number of times. At this signal, lines are formed at that precise number of children, no more and no less. To form the lines, the children stand side by side with their elbows locked. As soon as a line of the right number is formed, students begin to march to the music counterclockwise around the room. Any children left over go to the center of the circle and remain there until the next signal. On the next whistle or signal (a single blast) the lines break up, and all walk individually around the room in various directions.

Partner Stoop

Focus/Skill: Marching, body management

Procedure/Play: This activity follows the same rules and procedures as stooping as in circle stoop, but it is played with partners. The group forms a double circle, with partners facing counterclockwise which means that one partner is on the outside and one is on the inside. When the music begins, all march in the line of direction. After a short period of marching a signal (whistle) is sounded and the inside circle reverses direction and marches the other way – clockwise. The partners are thus separated. When the music stops, the other circle stands still, and the partners making up the inner circle walk to rejoin their respective outer circle partners.

Movement Activities 3-5

Sunday

Focus/Skills: Locomotor movements

Procedure/Play: Drawn 50 feet apart are two parallel lines. A player is "it" and stands in the center of the area between the two lines. All of the other students are on one of the two lines. The object is to cross to the other line without being tagged and without making a false start. Each line player stands with her front foot on the line. The line player must run across the line immediately. When the tagger calls "Sunday" anyone who does not run immediately is considered caught. The tagger can call other days of the week to confuse the runners. No player may make a start if another day of the week is called.

Squad Tag

Focus/Skill: Locomotor movements
Procedure/Play: An entire squad acts as taggers. The goal is to see which squad can tag the remaining class members in the shorter time. The tagging squad should wear pinnies. They stand in a football huddle formation in the center of the playing area. Their heads are down and their hands are joined in the huddle. The remainder of the class is scattered throughout the area. On command the tagging squad scatters and tags the other class members. When a class member is tagged, he/she steps in place and remains there. Each squad gets a turn to tag.
Teaching Idea: Children should be cautioned to watch for collisions, because there are children going in different directions. Students should stay within these boundaries.

Stealing Sticks

Focus/Skill: Locomotor movements
Equipment: Six to eight sticks, batons, or (any stick like objects) approximately 12 inches long.
Procedure/Play: The class is divided into two groups that are scattered on its own half of the playing area. Each team attempts to get to the opponents sticks without being tagged. If a player touches an opponents stick without being tagged, the stick may be bought

back safely to the player's own half of the playing area. Only one stick may be taken at a time. If tagged players go to their opponents prison. Prisoners may be rescued by teammates getting to the prison area without being tagged. The first player caught is the first player released. Only one prisoner may be released at a time. Once a player has gotten safely to the prison area, both are allowed to go back to their half of the playing area. The object is to try to be the team to get all of the opponent's sticks.

Teaching Idea: This game may be slow getting started because children are hesitant to cross over and get tagged. Children should be encouraged to use different strategies.

Maze Tag

Focus/Skill: locomotor skills.

Procedure/Play: The student's stand in rows that are aligned both from front to rear and from side to side. A runner and a chaser are chosen. The students all face the same way and join hands with the players on each side. The chaser tries to tag the runner, who runs between the rows with the restriction that he cannot break through or under the arms. The teacher can help the runner by calling "Right Face" or "Left Face" at the proper time. On command, two children drop hands, face the new direction, and grasp hands with those who are then on each side, thus making new passages available. When the runner is caught or when children become tired, new runners and chasers are chosen.

Stop and Start

Focus/Skill: Locomotor movements

Procedure/Play: The student's stand behind one of two goal lines, a leader stands off to the side, out of the path of the players. The leaders give a command, which utilizes the various locomotor skills, the children have learned. On this command the children execute desired movement (leap). When the teacher yells, "stop" all players must come to an immediate halt in place. Any player caught moving is sent back to the starting line. The first player to reach the opposite goal is the winner and new leader.

Balloon Tag

Focus/skill: Running, dodging
Equipment: Four to five balloons
Procedure/Play: To start, choose two students to be "it", they will strike the balloons, attempting to hit the other players and if successful will change places with the players hit. Players must remain within the boundaries of the playing area. Anyone running out of bounds to avoid getting caught will change places with the players chasing him/her. Any player hit with the balloon can avoid becoming "it" if he/she can catch the balloon before it touches the floor. If successful this player can tap the balloon away from "it".
Teaching Idea: Remind players to watch where they are running, not who is chasing them.

Push-Up Tag

Focus/Skill: Running, dodging
Procedure/Play: Chose two players to be 'it', the remaining players, spreading out, have to remain within the boundaries of the playing area. Once the game begins, players being chased are safe when they assume a push-up position for the count of three. If those who are "it" guard a player longer than 3 seconds the player is allowed to go free. Any player caught becomes the new "it".
Teaching Idea: Remind players to never jump over a player in the push-up position or push when they tag someone. Also issue pinnies and have four to five players be it.

Odd and Even Tag

Focus/Skill: Running, dodging.
Procedure/Play: The class is divided into half. The groups face

each other at half court. One team is designated Odd and the other team Even. The teacher stands between the groups and rolls the dice one at a time. If the sum is Odd, the odd team chases the even team toward its end of the wall. If the sum is even, the even team chases the odd group. For safety, cones are placed 10 feet from each end wall. Chased players making it past their cone are safe. Tagged players simply become members of the team that tagged them.

The Great Escape

Focus/Skill: Running, dodging
Equipment: Four pinnies, cones
Procedure/Play: Divide the class into five separate groups. One group stands in the middle of the floor (pinnies) while the other four move to separate corners. On command (whistle) students in each corner attempt escape to a different location without being tagged by one of students guarding the middle. Runners may simply run along a wall or cut diagonally across the middle. Runners have 10 seconds to leave their corner after they hear "go".

Non-locomotor

Capture the Flag

Focus/Skill: Bending, twisting, reaching, running, dodging.
Equipment: 2 "12" cones, 2 different color flags/pinnies for each end zone.
Procedure/Play: The class is divided into two halves; flags are placed on opposite ends of the playing area. The teams cannot cross the half-court line. They are safe as long as they remain on their side. The object of the game is to attempt to get to the other teams side, get their flag, and get back to their side without being tagged.

Indian Club

Focus/Skill: Non-locomotor movements
Equipment: Bowling pins, hula-hoop.
Procedure/Play: Students are divided into groups of four. Bowling pins (three) are set in a hula hoop for each group. The first player in each group runs and knocks pins down; the second player runs and stands pins up, one at a time. The object is to be the first team back to the starting position in order.

Barker's Hoopla

Focus/Skill: Non-locomotor movements.
Equipment: Hula hoops, beanbags
Procedure/Play: Arrange in each corner of the playing area, four hoops with one in the center of the playing area. Place five to six beanbags in each hoop. The class is divided into five equal teams, one group near each hoop. This is their home base. The object of the game is to steal beanbags from each other hoops and return them to the hoop that is home base for each team.

Teaching Idea: A player can take only one beanbag at a time, and must take it to home base and return before they can take another one. Beanbags cannot be thrown but must be physically placed in a home base hoop. No player can guard home base. Beanbags may be taken from any hoop. On command, to stop every player must freeze immediately.

Tagball

Focus/Skill: Non-locomotor skills
Equipment: Base, foam ball, playground ball.
Procedure/Play: A home line is drawn at one end of the playing area. A base or standard is placed 50 feet in front of the home line. Two teams are formed. One team is scattered around the fielding area, the boundaries of which are determined by the number of

children. The other team is lined up in single file behind the home line. The object of the game is for the fielding team to tag the runners with the ball. Two runners at a time try to round the base and head back for home without being tagged. The game is continuous, meaning that as a running team player is tagged or crosses the home line, another player starts immediately. The fielding team may run with the ball and pass it from player to player, trying to tag one of the runners. At the start of the game, the running team has two players ready at the right side of the home line. The others on the team are in line, waiting for a turn. The teacher throws the ball anywhere in the field, and the first two runners start toward the base. They must run around the base from the right side. After all of the players have run, the team exchange places.

Jump Ten Challenge

Focus/Skill: Non-locomotor movements
Equipment: Five beanbags, rubber discs per team or floor tape.
Procedure/Play: Teams line up along one sideline. Place the rubber discs every two feet and in a straight line in front of each team. Beanbags are placed on top of these discs. The first player on each team, using only one foot, will hop to the first beanbag, pick it up and return to the starting line. The beanbag is given to the next player in line. The player without touching any other body part to the floor continues doing this until he/she makes a mistake or picks up all five beanbags. The next player, in either case, will take his/her turn after the beanbags have been replaced. Teams continue to do this for ten minutes. The greatest total of beanbags picked up is the total to beat after the first player on each team has rotated one position to his/her right. After beanbags are replaced a new game is begun.

Over and Under

Focus/Skill: Bending, twisting, reaching.
Equipment: Playground ball

Procedure/Play: Players are in file formation, behind a starting line. The first player in each line has a ball. At the signal to start, the first player passes the ball over his/her head to the second player who passes it between his/her legs to the next player. The ball is passed over and under the whole time. The last player upon receiving the ball runs forward tot he front of the line and starts again. This is continued until the line is back in its original position with the ball in the hands of the original first player.

Manipulative Activities 3-5

Scatter

Focus/Skill: Throwing, catching
Equipment: Five nerf balls
Procedure/Play: Players are scattered throughout the playing area. They have three steps or five seconds to get rid of a ball. Players who are hit with a ball have to remember who hit them. Once the game starts, players are hit from the waist down, must go to either sideline and wait until the player who hit them is hit or they can hit someone with a ball from the sideline. If a player is hit from the sideline, not only the player throwing the ball but all those hit by the same player may re-enter the game. Players go to the sideline if they are hit from the waist down, or if they take more than three steps, hold the ball for five seconds, catch their own thrown balls, or run out of bounds.

Medic

Focus/Skill: Throwing, catching.
Equipment: Six to eight "8" gator-skin balls or some suitable foam, softball.
Procedure/Play: The class is divided into two groups, with each group designating one person as their medic. The area behind the end line is the hospital area in which the medic is safe. All balls are placed

on the centerline dividing each group's playing area. On signal, the players run up to the line, pick up a ball, take it back to their hospital area, and then move out to their half of the playing area. Each player throws the balls, attempting to hit as many opponents as possible below the waist or on the lower arms. Those hit squat down on the spot where they were hit, raise one hand, and call for the medic. The medic comes out from the hospital area and takes the player by the hand back to the hospital. The hit player may then return to the game. The game proceeds until time is called or until all the players on one team are hit, including the medic.

Teaching Ideas: The game may be modified by having the throwers considered hit if the opponents catch the balls thrown at them.

Five Pass

Focus/Skill: Catching, throwing

Equipment: One "8" inch foam ball, pinnies

Procedure/Play: One team begins with the ball. The object is to complete five passes without the ball touching the floor. The team without the ball attempts to intercept the ball or recover an incomplete pass. Each time a pass is completed, the team shouts the number of consecutive passes completed it represents. Each time a ball touches the floor or is intercepted, the count starts over. Players may not contact each other. Emphasis should be placed on spreading out and using the entire count area.

Teaching Suggestion: If players do not spread out, the area can be broken into quadrants and players restricted to the quadrants.

Bombs the Pins

Focus/Skill: Throwing

Equipment: 8 to 12 bowling pins per team, 10-12 foam rubber balls.

Procedure/Play: Teams are divided into halves, separated by a half-court line. The bowling pins are spaced directly in front of the line by each team. Each team has at least five balls. The object of the game is to knock over the other pins, not to throw at the opponent. Players throw the balls back and forth, they cannot cross the centerline. Whenever a pin is knocked over by a ball or player that club is removed. The goal is to be the team with the most pins standing at the end of the game. Out of bounds can be recovered but must be thrown from inside the court.

Teaching Ideas: Pins can be reset instead of removed.

Jolly Ball

Focus/Skill: Kicking
Equipment: 24-inch cage ball
Procedure/Play: In square formation are four team facing each other. Players sit in crab position, hands braced behind them. The members of each group are numbered consecutively. Each player waits until his number is called. A player (one from each team) move in crab position and try to kick the cage ball over any one of the three opposing teams goal line. The sideline players can also kick the ball. When a team allows a ball to go over its line, a new number is called for a new game.

Teaching Idea: Two players from each team can be called at the same time.

Whistle Ball

Focus/Skill: Catching, throwing
Equipment: A ball for groups of 6 to 8 players.
Procedure/Play: In circle formation eight or fewer children stand. A ball is passed rapidly back and forth among them in any order. The object is to be the player who stays in the game the longest. A player sits down in place if he/she makes any of the following mistakes: He/she has the ball when the whistle blows. (Teacher sets predetermined time). He/she makes a bad throw or fails to catch a good throw. He/she returns the ball directly to the person from whom it was received.

Hoop Lasso

Focus/Skill: Throwing
Equipment: Three cones and hoops for each team.
Procedure/Play: The class is divided into two to four teams, each team with a number from 1 to 6. There are three cones that are placed directly in front of each team five feet between them in a straight line. The game starts by the 1st player in each line throwing a hoop attempting to circle the 1st cone, as soon as the first cone has been circled, that player moves to the 2nd cone and the third cone. Each player gets three tries. Go until all have gone
Teaching Idea Have all players work together to finish in a set time.

Ball of Fire

Focus/Skill: Catching
Equipment: One trainer volleyball per group.
Procedure/Play: Students form groups standing in circles five feet from each other. The ball is volleyed, (using the set pass) to any other player in the circle. This person must catch the ball and then volley to another player and so on. As the ball is being volleyed and caught, teacher blows a whistle. The player who is in possession of the ball must sit down in the center of the circle while the others continues to volley until one person remains.
Teaching Idea: Use throwing and catching instead of volleying. Use two or more balls in each circle.

Odd Ball

Focus/Skill: Catching, throwing
Equipment: Seven trainer volleyballs
Procedure/Play: One team on each side of the net, with three or four balls in its possession. On a signal, each team throws the balls to the other team, and continues to do so as soon as they are caught. You want as few balls as possible on your side of the net at the end of the designated amount of time.

Body Management 3-5

Circle Hook On

Focus/Skill: Body management
Procedure/Play: One student plays against three others who form a small circle with joined hands. The object of the game is for the lone child to tag a designated player in the circle. The other two children in the circle, by dodging and maneuvering attempt to keep the tagger away from the third member of the circle. The circle players may maneuver and circle in any direction but must not release handgrips. The tagger, in attempting to touch the protected circle player, must go around the outside of the circle. She/he is not permitted to go underneath or through the joined hands of the circle players.
Teaching Idea: Watch for roughness by the two in the circle protecting the third.

Ocotopus

Focus/Skill: Body management
Procedure/Play: Octopus is a game that gets its name from the many hands joined together in the activity. The children stand shoulder to shoulder in a tight circle. Everyone thrusts the hands forward and reaches through the group of hands to grasp the hands across the circle. Players must make sure that they do not hold across the circle. Players may also not hold the hand of an adjacent player. The object is to untangle the mess created by the joined hands by going under, over or through fellow players. No one is permitted to release a handgrip during the unraveling. The end result should be one large circle or two smaller connected circles.
Teaching Idea: Two groups may compete against each other to see which can untangle first.

Jump and Bounce

Focus/skill: Body management
Equipment: A long jump rope, basketball
Procedure/Play: The group is divided into teams of six to eight members. The players on each team turn the rope while the other members take turn jumping into the middle of the turning rope. The first jumper bounces the ball once, the second jumper twice, etc. When the jumper fails to bounce the ball the required number of times, the next jumper starts with one bounce. A team inning consists of three jumping opportunities for each player.

Teaching suggestion: Use other hand skills while jumping such as tossing the ball in the air, passing to teammates.

Rope Cards

Focus/Skill: Body management
Equipment: Jump ropes, task cards
Procedure/Play: Design different tasks cards with rope activities that reinforce body management. Divide students into groups of five to seven students each. Have them complete task on each card. The groups rotate on a timed basis. Tasks:
   *Jump, hop- left foot, right foot, alternating feet.
   *Move along the floor in a designated pattern and backwards.
   *"Pepper" – turn the rope as rapidly as possible.
   *Jump rope moving in the opposite direction.
   *Cross and uncross arms.
   *Have one large rope with each partner turning an end- Jump two at once, Jump with half turns.

Balance

Focus/Skill: Body management
Procedure/Play: The class is standing on a black line, such as the half-court line in the gymnasium shoulder top shoulder

formation. The goal is to attempt to reverse the order of players in the line. Students cannot step off the line. The player who is last on the right end of the line should change places with the last player on the left of the line and so on and so on.

Classroom Activities

There will be times when physical education has to be conducted in the classroom. Procedures should be maintained so those program objectives are continued to be met.

Around the Row

Procedure: This game is played somewhat like musical chairs; this game involves the children from one row of a classroom and one extra player. All quietly walk around their row when the teacher gives the appropriate indication. "March" when the signal to stop is give, the children attempt to gain possession of one of the vacant seats. One player will be without a seat; he/she then proceeds across the room.

Beanbag Pitch

Beanbags and a small box (shoebox) for each team. Approximately two to six players line up behind a line, which is drawn ten to fifteen feet from a target box. Each player is allowed to take a specified number of pitches to hit the box. The score for each player is tallied and the team with the highest score wins.

Birds Fly

A student stands in front of the other children as the leader. He/she proceeds to call out the names of things that can fly (birds fly) and things that cannot fly (lions fly) always raising his/her arms in imitation of flying. The other children raise their arms only when the leader names something that can fly. If any child raises his arms when something is named that cannot fly, that child must sit down. The winner is that child who remains standing the longest.

Bicycle Race

One half of the class is used, allowing alternate rows to perform one at a time. Each child stands in the aisle between two desks one hand on his own desk and his other hand on the neighboring desk. On a signal from the teacher, the child supports himself on his hands while bicycling with his legs. The child who is able to bicycle the longest without allowing his feet to touch the floor is the winner.

Boiler Burst

The children are grouped around a player who begins a story. When he/she calls "Boiler Burst" this is the signal that he is going to chase the other players who run for the safety zone. The first player caught starts the game again, with the player around him. The same story may be continued or a new one begins.

Bowling

Bowling pins and balls are needed. Using an aisle of the classroom as an alley, the pins are placed at one end of the row. A ball of adequate size is used to roll down the 'alley' to hit the target. Competition can be between rows, squads, or individuals.

Caged Lion

One player is selected to be the lion and takes his/her position on hands and knees inside the tem foot square that has been designated inside the classroom. The other players run up to the 'lion' and through his cage tempting him. The 'lion' tries to reach out and tag anyone of the players tempting him. Should a player be tagged by the 'lion', that player takes the place of the 'lion' in the cage.

Cat and Mice

One student who is selected to be the cat sits with his back to the other players, who sit in their seats. The teacher chooses four or five mice and signals for them to quietly sneak up to the cats hiding place and scratch on the desks or stools. This is a signal for the cat to chase the mice back to the safety of their holes (desks). If tagged, the mouse becomes a cat; if more than one is tagged, the first tagged becomes the cat. If no one is tagged, that same child is the cat again. New children are chosen to be mice and the game begins again.

Change Seats

With all the children seated in their seats the teacher commands "change left" "change right", "change front", "change back". The children shift in the direction named, quickly and quietly. If the shift is forward, those in the front row stand until commanded to "change back". If the command is to shift right, those in the right hand row of seats stand, and so on.

Lost Children

The child who is "it" leaves the room. While he/she is gone, the rest of the children leave their seats and walk around the room. When "it" returns the teacher says, "The children are lost". Please lead them safely home". "It" then tries to seat the children in their own places. The object is to see how many he can seat correctly.

O'Grady Says

One player is chosen as the leader. He/she stands in the aisles facing the leader. The leader gives commands, some of which are prefaced by :O'Grady says" and some of which are not. Any player who makes a mistake by not doing a command not preceded by "O'Grady says" must sit down in his seat if the leader sees the error and calls his name. After the leader has caught three players making errors, another leader is selected.

Simon Says

Select one student as the leader. They stand in the front of the room and the other players stand in the aisles facing the leader. The leader gives commands, some are prefaced by "Simon says" and some are not. The players must do everything commanded which is preceded by "Simon says' they must not obey a command which is not preceded by "Simon says". Any player who makes a mistake must sit down in their seat if the leader catches three players' errors another leader is selected. The three players get into the game again. The game starts again with the new leader giving the commands.

Trash Can Basketball

The squads are designated as teams, with each individual taking a turn to have a shot at a trashcan that has been placed 5- 10 feet away against a wall. An 8-inch nerf ball or softball can be used. As the games goes on increase the number of shots each player can take. Award a point for each basket made and compare the scores among the squads.

Wellness Activities

Wellness is an important part of the physical education curriculum. It provides children with knowledge and skills that are necessary to carry out and sustain an effective comprehensive fitness program. The wellness model includes teaching children how to identify various body parts, understanding how eating and exercising go hand in hand, how physical inactivity and obesity are related and how to use effective coping and decision making skills.

Body Tag

Grade level: k-2
Focus/skill: Throwing and catching
Objective: Identification of body parts.
Equipment: Fleece balls or soft foam balls for throwing.
Procedure/Play: As prerequisite students are given a picture of a skeleton that has been labeled in big letters the following body parts: arm, hand, shoulder and leg. The teacher goes over the handout with the class pronouncing each word and having that student demonstrate by pointing to that part.

The class then play a game that reinforces what they just went over by dividing into two groups with one group (taggers) wearing the pinnies, the taggers will attempt to tag the opposing group with a fleece ball. The tag has to hit the player on one of the body parts that have been identified or it does not count. The ball has to be thrown at the other player not touched. When tagged, students must freeze and can only be freed by a teammate. Continue three to five minutes then switch.

Vegetable March

Grade level: K-2
Focus/skill: Locomotor movement
Objective: Understanding how eating and exercising go hand in hand.
Equipment: For each child a picture of laminated fruit or vegetable.
Procedure/Play: The class is in circle formation with each student standing on a picture of a fruit or vegetable. These are used as poly spot markers. On signal the students will walk around moving from poly spot to poly spot. On the next signal they stop. Whoever lands on that particular spot removes that spot, names the fruit or vegetable and sits in the middle of that circle. This continues until it goes down to the last two.
Teaching Idea: Change the locomotor movement, hop, leap, etc.

Busy Bee

Grade level: k-2
Focus/Skill: Locomotor movement
Objective: Identification of body parts.
Procedure/Play: The children are scattered with partners in the playing area, with one extra person who is their leader. The leader calls the names of a body part, such as "back to back", "knee to knee", and so forth, the partners match those parts named. When the leader calls "Busy bee" each person finds a new partner. The one without a partner becomes the new leader.
Teaching Idea: Emphasize listening carefully to the leader. Encourage the children to think of as many different body parts as possible.

Cigarette Tag

Grade level: 3-5
Focus/skill:Locomotor movements
Objective: Understanding how eating and exercising go hand in hand.
Procedure/Play: As a prerequisite students have been introduced to the ill-effects of smoking (cancer, asthma, etc.) Place one cigarette (student) in the middle of the floor. Following a signal to begin, the cigarette attempts to chase and tag the rest of the class. Each person tagged chain up with the cigarette by placing his/her hands on the person hips. As soon as four or five students are tagged, it becomes harder and harder for the pack to move. The analogy is that the more you smoke, the slower you run.

Cholesterol Tag

Grade level: 3-5
Objective: Understanding how physical activity and obesity are related.
Focus/Skill: Locomotor skills.
Procedure/Play: Students are divided into two groups on opposite ends of the floor. Select two students (cholesterol) to stand in the middle of the room. Explain that all of the runners are BLOOD trying to get to the HEART (opposite walls) without being tagged by the cholesterol. Each time that blood is tagged, it becomes part of the cholesterol. Soon the middle is filled with cholesterol and blood has a difficult time making it to the heart. This analogy is that cholesterol blocks the passage of blood.

Risk Tag

Grade level: 3-5
Focus/skill: Locomotor movements
Equipment: Five Cause cards 5 softball bases.

Objective: Understanding how physical inactivity and obesity are related.

Procedure/Play: As prerequisite students should have been introduced to the dangers of smoking. Have each student stand in his/her personal space. Place one of the following risk factors signs and a related cause card under each of five softball bases spread across the playing area. Next, designate three taggers who will attempt to tag as many classmates as possible. Tagged players must run to the closest base, and pick up and read the cause card before reentering the game.

Bases Cause Cards

Smoking daily smokers have a 50% higher chance of heart attack.
Obesity raises blood pressure and harms circulation.
Inactivity increases the risk of heart disease and obesity.
Diet fatty junk foods are high in sugar and contribute to obesity.
Alcohol contributes to levels of fat in the blood.
Food Chain
Grade level: k-2
Focus/skill: Locomotor movements
Objective: Understanding how physical inactivity and obesity are related.

Procedure/Play: Review with the children how healthy and regular exercise can help to maintain weight, make you stronger, and look and feel better. Then have students stand in their personal space with eyes closed. Teacher walks by and whispers one of the following in each person's ear (apple, carrot, banana, broccoli). On signal, students place palms up (safety bumpers) and walk slowly forward shouting their particular food choice. As similar choices encounter, they grab hands and rhythmically shout their food attempting to attract all of the other "same foods" to their line. Which group can form their FOOD CHAIN first?

Teaching Idea: Remind them to keep their eyes closed.

Get Healthy

Grade level: k-5
Focus/skill: Running, tagging
Equipment: 100 large index cards
Objective: Understanding how eating and exercising go hand in hand.
Procedure/Play: On one side of 50 index cards write the name of a different junk food e.g. candy bar, soda, chocolate cake etc. On the other 50 cards, print healthier alternatives, such as carrot, apple, broccoli, etc. To assist younger students, circle the junk foods.
Students are arranged in lines of three along one sideline. Cards are scattered face down across the floor. Following a signal to begin, the first person in each line runs out and turns over one card. If the card is a healthy choice it is returned to the head of that teams line. Junk foods are replaced (facedown) and that player returns empty handed and tags the next player in line. Only ONE CARD can be picked up per trip. The teams collecting more than eight healthy choices in two minutes gain a point.

The Challenge

Grade level: 3-5
Focus/skill: Non locomotor activities
Equipment: 1 81/2' playground ball for every player, 8 cones and 3 hurdles.
Objective: Coping skills, decision making, cooperation
Procedure/Play: Class is divided into three teams. A line is placed ten feet in front of the end line. The first player stands on the line, with the others behind him or her in file formation. The players on each team have a ball pressed against their chests and backs. The first in line has a ball pressed against their back and holds a ball. The last player presses his/her ball against the back of the next player in line. Pressure has to be applied to keep balls from falling. Time the activity. On signal, each team has to zigzag through the cones, and return. Players may not use their hands once the ball has been placed

between players. The team must stop and replace any ball that falls to the ground. The team starts over when a player touches the ball with a hand, except to replace it. Exception – players may reposition their balls when they pass the far cone. Teams do not have to go around or over the obstacles when returning.

Teaching Idea: Remind the players how important it is to keep a straight line. The best way for a player to do this is to look at the back of the head of the player in front of them.

Try Me

Grade level: -5
Focus/skill: Non-locomotor and locomotor activities
Equipment: Balloons, hula-hoops, and playground balls.
Objective: Decision-making skills, coping skills, and cooperation.
Procedure/play: players are divided equally into 4 teams. Any number of challenges can be created for players to try.
1. How long can you keep a rainbow ball in the air?
Can an entire group, holding hands, move a hoop around a circle in a set time limit?
Can you move two hoops, on opposite sides of a circle, and have one overtake the other?
How many balls can two players carry across a gymnasium?
Can an entire team, holding hands; cross an open area touching one body part less than the number going?

Relay Races

Relay races can help children to cooperate since they demand that teammates follow rules and directions.
Relays using beanbags
Beanbag Pass Relay
Procedure/play: Players are in a line, standing side by side. The player on the right starts the beanbag, which is passed from one player to the next down the line. When it gets to the end of the line,

the relay is over. The teacher should be sure that each player handles the bag. Children should rotate positions in line.

Circle Beanbag Pass Relay

Procedure/play: Players stand in a circle facing out. But close enough so that the beanbag can be handled from player to player. One circuit begins and ends with the same player. The under leg pass can be used in this formation also.

Carry and Fetch Relay

Procedure/play: Players are closed squad formation, with a hoop or circle positioned up to 30 feet in front of each team. The first runner on each team has a beanbag. On command "Go" this player carries the beanbag forward and puts it inside the hoop; then she/he returns and tags off the next runner. The second runner goes forward picks up the beanbag and hands it off to the third runner. One runner carries the beanbag forward and the next runner fetches it back. Different locomotor movements can be specified.

Arch Ball Relay

Procedure/play: A ball is for each team. The first player in the line hands ball over to the next player in line. This continues until the ball reaches the end. When the end player receives the ball, he/she runs to the head of the line and passes the ball back again. When the original head of the line returns, the relay is over.

Bounce Ball Relay

Procedure/play: A circle is drawn 10-15 feet in front of each team. The first player goes to the circle, bounces the ball once, and returns the ball to the second player who repeats the same routine. The last player on the team carries the ball over the finish line.

Galloping Relay

Procedure/play: One player at a time gallops to a turning point and returns tags the next player in line. The object is to be the first team to have all the players back in original starting position.

Teaching Idea: Use various locomotor movements.

Polo Stick Relay

Procedure/play: Pretend to be a pogo stick by keeping a stiff body and jumping on the toes. Students hold their hands in front of them

as if grasping the stick. Students go one at a time until all have gone.
Run Up Walk Back Relay
Procedure/Play: One player at a time runs up to a starting point and walks back. The goal is to be the first team to have all players back in original starting position.
Walking Relay
Procedure/play: One player at a time walks to a turning point and back. The first team to have all players back in original starting position gets to start the next relay.
Lanes Relay
Procedure/Play: The teams are in lane formation. The first player run forward to a designated point and circles the cone, comes back and tags the next person in line, goes to the end of the line and kneels down. Continue until all have gone. The object is to be the first team to have all players squatting down.
Relays Grade level 3-5
Partner Relay
Procedure/play: The class is divided into three to four teams. The first player runs forward, touches cones that has been set at a designated distance at opposite end of playing area and comes back to team. He/she then holds hands with next player in line and both goes to cone at other end. The first player stays, the second player returns holds hands with the third player in line, goes to the cone at the opposite end. The second stays, the third person goes back to the other end and takes the hand of the fourth player and goes to the cone at the opposite end. Continue until all have gone. Each player must remember to always come back and get someone. The last player goes down with their partner but must return to the cone at the opposite end and back, this is how the race is ended.
Pass and Squat Relay
Procedure/play: A player (number 1) with a ball stands behind a line 10 feet in front of his teammates, who are in lane formation. Number 1 passes the ball to number 2, who returns the ball to no. 1. As soon as he has returned the ball to the no. 1 no. 2 squats down so that the throw can be made to no 3 and so on down the line. When the

last person in line receives the ball, she does not return it but carries it forward straddling the members of his/her team, including no. 1 who has taken the place at the head of the line. The player carrying the ball forward then acts as the passer. The relay is over when the original no 1 player receives the ball in the back position and straddles the player to return to his original position.

Circle Dribbling Relay

Procedure/play: Two basketballs are used. Two teams each form a large circle standing three yards apart and facing in. One player starts dribbling the ball around the circle weaving in and out between players. After the players complete the circle he/she passes tot he player ahead of him who repeats the performance.

Figure Eight Dribbling Basketball Relay

Procedure/play: Two basketballs, six bowling pins are needed. The three bowling pins are placed in a line about five yards apart and five yards in front of each team. The first player must run up tot he pins, dribble in and out of them in the path of a figure 9. The player must then run back and give the ball to the second player who repeats the process.

Sack Race

Procedure/play: Either lane or shuttle formation can be used. The sacked runner goes around a cone, returns to the team, and gives the sack to the next participant. Continue until all have gone. This is a good field day activity.

Run the Bases Relay

Procedure/play: There are four white bases and four orange bases for the other team. There are eight teams with three players on each team. Bases are arranged in figure eight design and are arranged approximately 40 feet apart. The first runner on each team will stand on the base. On command, the first one in line will run the bases in number order, based on where he/she is starting. The next runner may leave when the one in front has passed the team's base before continuing. Any player passing another runner may bypass the next base. but must continue running the same pattern. A team is finished when every person has completed five turns. The time of the first team finished is the time to beat in the next race.

Sport skills k-5
Basketball Skills
Passing

Chest pass
Hands are placed behind the ball.
Thumbs pointed down and back.
Keeping ball at chest level, extend arms forward.
Step forward with one foot and flick wrists forward.
Ball received at chest level.

Two Hand Bounce pass
Assume stance as if making chest pass.
Hands behind ball, fingers spread, thumbs pointed downward.
Ball hits the floor at least three-fourth of distance to the receiver.

Wrap-a- round bounce pass
Player is in Triple Threat Position.
Fakes pass high, steps to side and slightly around.
Left foot (pivot foot) remains stable shielding defender.
Low bounce pass is made around defender.

Two handed Overhead Pass
Hold the ball overhead with hands on each side.
Fingers spread, take one step forward
Extend arms with snap of wrist.
Pass is made over a defender to its' intended target.
Follow through path of the ball.
SHOOTING
Lay Up
Aim for square right above basket.
Step on opposite foot.
With the other leg, raise the knee and jump up toward basket.
Extend shooting arm for bank off of backboard.

Return to the floor with caution.
JUMP SHOT
Hold ball overhead, shooting hand placed behind ball and under it.
Knees slightly bent, one foot forward.
Jump off both feet and shoot at peak of jump, full extension of shooting arm upward and forward. Using good wrist action.
Medium arc on the ball.

Pivoting
Pivot
Come to a complete stop.
The pivot foot stays intact.
The other foot is moved forward.

Reverse pivot
Pivot foot does not leave the floor.
Other foot is turned and moved backward.
Guarding
Knees are slightly bent.
One foot ahead of the other.
Hands are up, in ready position.
Maintains good balance.

Dribbling
Stance is low.
Use the fingerpads not fingertips to control the basketball.
Keep ball close to the body as you dribble.
Maintain dribble so that it does not bounce above waist.

Soccer

Passing

Pass using the outside of the foot
One foot is placed beside and slightly away from the ball.

Knees are slightly bent, eyes on the ball.
Toes are pointed in the direction of target.
Contact is made using laces of the shoe.
Follow through is made in direction of kick.

Pass using instep of foot
Place non-kicking foot beside the ball.
Knees bent, eyes on the ball.
Kicking leg is swung back.
Contact is made using the inside of the foot.
Follow-through with leg in path of the ball.
Dribbling
Head up.
Contact the ball using the side of the foot.
Ball is kept in front of the body for control.
The ball is tapped for movement.

Trapping
Get in the path of the ball.
Stop the ball by placing the bottom of your foot on top of the ball.

Use the other leg for support and balance.

Throw-In
Feet are together, planted firmly to ground.
One hand is on each side of the ball.

Ball is brought back behind head.

Thumbs pointing back, arms bent at the elbow.

With both feet in contact with the ground, ball is released
overhead.
Volleyball
Ready Position

Feet are placed in front of the other.
Weight is on balls of the feet.
Arms are at the side.

Passing
Overhead Pass or Volley
Knees bent.
Get body underneath ball.
Hands held at forehead level.
Fingers spread and elbows out.
Contact is made using fingers not palms.
Follow through with hands and arms after hitting the ball.
Forearm Pass
Move quickly to spot where ball is heading.
Place one foot slightly in front of the other.
Lean forward with hands together, fingers intertwined, thumbs touching.
Forearms extended out from body.
Contact is made with fists or forearms.
The hip, knees and elbows are flexed.
Follow through in the direction of hit.

Underhand Serve
Stride forward with foot that is opposite of serving hand.
Ball is held below the waist and out from the body.
Arm is bought back and contacts is made on ball at waist level.
Follow through in direction serve is made.

Floor Hockey
Ready Position
Stick is on ground flat side down.
Place hand at top of the stick and pick stick up as if you are "shaking hands with the stick".
Approximately six to nine inches below that hand comfortably place other hand.

Feet slightly apart keep stick low to ground.
DRIBBLING
Get in ready position.
Head up, good grip on stick.
Lean forward keeping ball or puck in front of body.
Contact is made using tapping motion in a side to side matter.
PASSING
In ready position hold stick firmly.
Head down, eyes on ball stick at waist level.
Weight is shifted from back to front foot.
In a sweeping motion, contact is made striking through the puck.
Stick should not go above the knees.

Appendix A

Sample Physical Education Lesson Plan Thematic Model
Content: Science
Theme:
Circulatory SystemLevel:
Developmental 3-5
Standard: *Personal Health and Fitness
Topic: *Educational game: "Risk Tag"
Focus/Skill: Locomotor movements
Objective: Understanding how physical inactivity and obesity are related.

Participants: Up to 25
Equipment: Bases and Cause cards
Procedure/Description: As prerequisite students should have been introduced to the dangers of smoking through classroom teacher. Have each student stand in his/her personal space. Place one of the following risk factors signs and a related cause card under each of five softball bases spread across the playing area. Next, designate three taggers who will attempt to tag as many classmates as possible. Tagged players must run to the closest base, and pick up and read the cause card before reentering the game.

Bases Cause Cards
Smoking daily smokers have a 50% higher chance of heart attack.

Obesity raises blood pressure and harms circulation. Inactivity increases the risk of heart disease and obesity. Diet fatty junk foods are high in sugar and contribute to obesity.

Alcohol contributes to levels of fat in the blood

***Benchmark: Recognizes that physiological responses to exercise are associated with

their own levels of fitness.

Teaching Idea: Teacher can have poster/chart size diagram of human body to make it easier for students to understand.

Safety Statement: Students should be careful when running and tagging.

Evaluation/Closure: Check for understanding by question and answer session.

*19 New York State Learning Standards for Health, Physical Education and Family and Consumer Sciences

**20 Turner & Turner, 2000, Ready to use pre-sport skills activities program

***1 Moving into the Future, National Standards for Physical Education, (NASPE) 2004

Appendix B

Sample Physical Education Lesson Plan Thematic Model
Content: Math
Theme: counting with numbers
Level: 3-5
Standard: *A safe and healthy environment
Topic: Educational games "Twenty One"
Focus/Skill: shooting, ball control
Objective: Student will practice dribbling and shooting skills
Student will relate the concept of counting to grouping and place value
Participants: Up to 25
Procedure/Description: Players are in file formation or separated by squads. The first player in each line has a basketball per goal. Each player is permitted two shots from any where in the lane. Each shot counts as a point. After they shoot the basketball they are to retrieve it and dribble to next person in line, who is moving towards the person who is dribbling. The dribbler stops and makes the pass and goes to the end of the line. The next player receives the pass and takes his turn. The object is to see how long it takes a group to reach 21. As each team scores a point, they have to yell out in unison the number of baskets they have made thus when getting to 21 shouting it out.

*Benchmark: Dribbles then passes a basketball to a moving object

Safety Statement: Students should never pass the ball to someone who is not looking.

Evaluation/Closure: Check for understanding

*19 New York State Learning Standards for Health, Physical Education, and Family and Consumer Sciences

**1 Moving into the Future, National Standards for Physical Education (NAPSE) 2004

Appendix C

Sample Physical Education Lesson Plan Shared Integration Model

Content: Math

Theme: Number identification; time.

Level: 3-5

Standard: *Personal Health and Fitness

Topic: Fitness testing

Focus/Skill: locomotor and nonlocomotor movements

Objective: Student will perform physical fitness activities.

Student will demonstrate the concept of time, distance through problems related to actual situations.

Participants: up to 25

Procedure/Play: Mark two parallel lines 30 feet apart and place two blocks of wood or similar object behind one of the lines. Students start behind opposite line. To start the student runs to the blocks, picks one up, runs back to the starting line, places block behind the line, runs back and picks up the second block, and runs back across starting line. Have student's pair up and time each other with a stopwatch, while the teacher records the time.

**Benchmark: Engages in appropriate physical activity that results in the development of cardiovascular endurance.

Safety Statement: Students be careful when running.

Evaluation/Closure: Were there any injuries? Check for understanding.

*19 New York State Learning Standards for Health, Physical Education and Family and
Consumer Sciences
** 1 Moving into the Future, National Standards for Physical Education, (NAPSE) 2004

Appendix D

Sample Physical Education Lesson Plan: Shared
Integration Model
Discipline: Language Arts/P.E.

Concept: Spelling

Level: k-2

Standard: *A safe and healthy environment

Topic: Educational games, cooperation and spelling

Focus/skill: passing, trapping soccer skills

Objective: Student will practice soccer passing and
trapping skills.
Student will work on spelling skills.

Participants: up to 25

Procedure/Description: Students are spread throughout playing
area with a Soccer ball and a partner. They should have a list of the

spelling words from their classroom teacher. They pass the soccer ball to their partner saying a letter as they pass the ball. The partner says a letter as they stop or trap the ball, they are trying to successfully spell out the word they were given.

**Benchmark: Taps the soccer ball forward using the big toe area of the inside foot.

Safety Statement: Student should be careful when kicking the ball.

Evaluation/Closure: Check for understanding.

*19 New York State Learning Standards for Health, Physical Education, and Family and
Consumer Sciences
**1 Moving into the Future, National Association for Sport and Physical Education (NAPSE) 2004

Appendix E

Sample Physical Education Lesson Plan

Level:

State Standard:

Topic:

Focus/Skill:

Objective:

Participants:

Procedure/Play:

Benchmark:

Teaching Idea:

Safety Statement:

Evaluation/Closure:

Appendix F

Equipment List

This is a basic supply list that should be devised with the notion that every child has a piece of equipment.

Balloons
Balls,
Basketballs, mini and juniors sizes
Beach balls, all sizes
Cage ball 24 inch, with additional bladders in stock.
Fleece
Footballs, foam, nerf, mini and junior sizes.
Gator skin, all sizes
Playground, all sizes
Soccer, 3, 4 and 5 size
Softball sets including masks and batting helmets
Sponge
Tennis
Volleyball trainers
Whiffle
Batons (for relays)
Batting Tees

Beanbags, various sizes, colors, shapes
Bowling sets
Cones, all sizes
Fitness dice
Flags for tagging
Hockey sets, foam and plastic
Hula-hoops, all sizes
Indian clubs
Ropes,
Jump ropes
Single
Partner
Double Dutch
Jump the shot
Tug-o-war
Lacrosse sets
Parachutes, small and large sizes
Pinnies, various sizes and colors
Scoops
Scooters (Gymnasium)
Spot markers

Appendix G

ASSESSMENTS

Student Self Evaluation
Level: k-2

Manipulative Skills Task card: Tossing

Name_____

Grade_____

Teacher_____

Can You?

Toss a ball straight up and catch it 8 out of 10 times.
Toss the ball straight up, touch the floor, and catch it 9 out
of 10 times.

Toss the ball in the air and catch it with your non-dominate hand 7 out of 10 times.

Touch the ball straight up, sit down, and catch it 8 out of 10 times

Teacher_____

When you have completed the task, check them off or seek the teacher to determine if the criteria have been met.

Appendix H

Teacher Observation

Softball Skill Analysis

Name_____

Grade_____

Skill: Batting

O Keep your hands together.

O Bat is held over right shoulder, pointing back and up.

O Swing the bat at the height of the pitch.

O Swing through the ball.

O Follow through after contact (hit) is made.

Skill Analysis Appendix I

Physical Fitness Testing (Presidential)

	Age	Curl-ups or (# one minute)	Partial Curl-ups (#)	Shuttle Run (seconds)	V-sit Reach (inches) or	Sit and Reach (centi meters)	One Mile Run Min/ Sec	Pull Ups # or	Rt. Angle Push-ups
	6	33	22	12.1	+3.5	31	10:15	2	9
	7	38	24	11.5	+3.5	30	9:22	4	14
Boys	8	40	30	11.1	+3.0	31	8:48	5	17
	9	41	37	10.9	+3.0	31	8:31	5	18
	10	45	35	10.3	+4.0	30	7:57	6	22
	11	47	43	10.0	+4.0	31	7:32	6	27
	12	50	64	9.8	+4.0	31	7:11	7	31
	13	53	59	9.5	+3.5	33	6:50	7	39
	14	56	62	9.1	+4.5	36	6:26	10	40
	15	57	75	9.0	+5.0	37	6:20	11	42
Boys	16	56	73	8.7	+6.0	38	6:08	11	44
	17	55	66	8.7	+7.0	41	6:06	13	53
	6	32	22	12.4	+5.5	32	11:20	2	9
	7	34	24	12.1	+5.0	32	10:36	2	14
	8	38	30	11.8	+4.5	33	10:02	2	17
Girls	9	39	37	11.1	+5.5	33	9:30	2	18
	10	40	33	10.8	+6.0	33	9:19	3	20
	11	42	43	10.5	+6.5	34	9:02	3	19
	12	45	50	10.4	+7.0	36	8:23	2	20
	13	46	59	10.2	+7.0	38	8:13	2	21
	14	47	48	10.1	+8.0	40	7:59	2	20
Girls	15	48	38	10.0	+8.0	43	8:08	2	20
	16	45	49	10.1	+9.0	42	8:23	1	24
	17	44	58	10.0	+8.0	42	8:15	1	25

Student Portofolio's   Appendix J

SOCIAL IQ

Name: _____
Grade: _____
Room: _____

Rating

Criteria	Needs Improvement	Most Often	Always
*Follows directions			
*Self-directed			
*Cooperates with others			
*Sportsmanship			

Comments:

[20] Ready to Use Pre-Sport Skills Activities Program by Turner and Turner Parker Publishing, 2000

Student Portofolio's Appendix J

SOCIAL IQ
Name: _____
Grade:_____
Room:_____

Rating

Criteria   Needs Improvement   Most Often   Always

*Follows directions

*Self-directed

*Cooperates with others

*SportsmanshComments:

20 Ready to Use Pre-Sport Skills Activities Program by Turner and Turner Parker Publishing, 2000

Student Portfolio Appendix K

Physical Education Contract

Name_____

Grade_____
    Classroom Teacher_____

I promise I will try to actively participate at all times. I will

show respect and consideration for others. I will use the

equipment and supplies in a safe manner. I will follow the

directions of the teacher, staying on task.

Student Signature_____

Parent/Guardian Signature_____

Date_____

Appendix L

Parental Report

Physical Education Progress Report

Name_____

Grade/Teacher_____

Marking Period____ Start_____ end_____

To be handed out every 3 weeks.

Send copy (1) home (2) file (3) Classroom teacher

Student Portfolio

Appendix M

Student Journal

Name
Grade
Teacher

Date of Entry _____

Please write in your journal your accounts of the past week in physical education class. Please be sure to include what you learned this week, activities you think you would like to try, what you think you improved at, as well as the activity you think you need to work on.

References

1. National Association for Sport and Physical Education (2004). Moving into the future: National standards for physical education (2nd ed.). Reston, VA: Author.

2. Langford, G.A. & Carter, L. (2003). Academic excellence must include physical education. *The Physical Educator, 60,* (1) 28-33.

3. Pangrazi, R.P., Corbin, C.B., & Welk, G.J. (1998). Physical activity for children. *Journal of physical education, recreation and dance, 67,* (4) 38-43.

4. Summerfiled, L.M. (1998). *Promoting physical activity and exercise among children.* (Report No. RR93002015). Washington, DC: ERIC Clearinghouse on Teaching and Teacher Education. ERIC Document Reproduction Service No. ED416204.

5. Physical Activity and Health: A Report of the Surgeon General. (1999). Atlanta, GA: U.S. Department of Health and Human Services, Centers for Disease Control and Prevention.

6. United States Department of Health and Human Services, Healthy People 2010. Understanding and Improving Health 2nd eds. Washington, DC: U.S. Government Printing Office, November, 2000.

7. Encarta Encyclopedia, Retrieved June 2005, from http:// encarta.msn.com

8. Benton, D., & Parker, P.Y. (1998). Breakfast, blood glucose and cognition. American Journal of Clinical Nutrition, 67 (4) supp. 772s-778s.

9. Scheuer, L.J., & Mitchell, D. (2003). Does physical activity influence academic performance? Retrieved June 2005 from The New P.E. and Sports Dimension newsletter http://www-sports-media.org/sportapolisnewsletter19.htm.

10. Elliott, E., & Sanders S. (2002). Keep children moving: Promoting physical activity throughout the curriculum. Retrieved June 2005 from PBS Teacher Source www.PBS.org.

11. Samuels, C.A. (1999). Gym class shapes up for a new generation. Washington Post 1999 Apr. 12: A1

12. Fukushima, R. (1999). P.E. makeover: St. Paul Pioneer Press; Sept. 13 8E.

13. Pangrazi, R.P., & Dauer, V.P. (1992). Dynamic physical education for elementary school children (10th eds.). Macmillan, NY.

14. Thomas, K.T., Lee, A.M., & Thomas J.R. (2003). Physical education methods for elementary teachers (2nd eds.). Human Kinetics, Champlain, IL.

15. Hastad, D.N., & Lacy, A.C. (1998). Measurement and Evaluation in physical education and exercise science. (3rd eds). Allyn & Bacon, MA.

16. Nichols, B. (1990). Moving and learning: the elementary school physical education experience. Times Mirror/Mosby College, St. Louis, MO.

17. Carpenter, J., & Tunnell, D. (1994). Elementary P.E.Teachers Survival Guide.Parker Publishing, West Nyac, NY.

18. Hale, B., & Franks, B. (2001). Get fit, a handbook for youth ages 6-17, how to meet the presidents challenge. US Department of Human Services, Presidents Council on Physical Fitness and Sports.

19. New York State Learning Standards for Health, Physical Education, and Family and Consumer Sciences http://www.nysatl.nysed.gov/standards.html

20. Turner, L.F., & Turner, S. (2000). Ready to use pre-sport skills activities program. Parker Publishing, West Nyac, NY.

Breinigsville, PA USA
18 January 2010
230965BV00002B/75/A